Fables from India

THE
BEGINNING
OF THE
MAHABHARATA

AND
OTHER STORIES

Other Titles in the *Fables from India* Series

A Crocodile Makes History and Other Stories
The Happy Monk and Other Stories
The Pillar of Justice and Other Stories

Fables from India

THE
BEGINNING
OF THE
MAHABHARATA

AND
OTHER STORIES

BASED ON
INDIAN AFTER DINNER STORIES BY
A.S. PANCHAPAKESA AYYAR

COMPILED AND EDITED BY
TERRY O'BRIEN

RUPA

Published by
Rupa Publications India Pvt. Ltd 2013
7/16, Ansari Road, Daryaganj
New Delhi 110002

Sales centres:
Allahabad Bengaluru Chennai
Hyderabad Jaipur Kathmandu
Kolkata Mumbai

ISBN: 978-81-291-2072-4

10 9 8 7 6 5 4 3 2 1

Typeset by Innovative Processors, New Delhi

Contents

Introduction

India is a land of myriad colours. With its rich history of folklore, India abounds in stories that have enthralled readers from time immemorial.

The oral tradition of narrating stories has ensured that these stories have been passed down from generation to generation. This exciting collection brings together a few of these classic tales for the young reader.

Jealous Husband Taught a Lesson

Sri Krishna was the darling of Brindaban. All the ladies of the place were mad about him. They were irresistibly attracted to the divine youth, and spent the evenings dancing with him in the glades on the banks of the Yamuna. For hours they danced like this, in union with the Infinite, to the music of the spheres and the even more delightful music from the Lord's flute. They forgot their husbands, their homes, their worries and even their children.

Sundari was one of those ladies. She lived with her husband Kittu and mother-in-law Pattu in a dark ill-ventilated house smelling of stale butter and cockroaches. Her husband was a fat, unprepossessing cowherd, only good at milking cows and not at all at any of the fine arts or even at making love to his fair wife. But Sundari, like a Hindu wife, loved him devotedly, and he returned her love.

Sundari, however, loved to leave him and the cows behind for a while, for the twilight and moonlight dances on the banks of the blue Yamuna. Kittu and Pattu did not like this at all. Sternly, they asked her to desist. 'This is immodest. That horrible wretch ought to be punished. Simply because he is the son of our chief he should not play havoc with all our girls,' said Kittu to Pattu. Pattu heartily agreed. 'Oh, the Lord does not want us. It is we who want the Lord,' said Sundari to them. 'What joy does the stone feel on which cows scratch themselves? It is the cows who get relief, not the stone. What joy does the Yamuna get by allowing the boats to float on it? It is the boats which are moved on.' 'We don't want all this sophistry. I forbid you to go there,' said Kittu. 'Mother,' said he to Pattu, 'See also that Krishna does not sneak into our home assuming some disguise or other. He is very clever at assuming different forms.' 'I shall see to that,' said Pattu. 'I shall sit behind the door and cudgel him well if he tries to play his tricks on me.' Then Kittu left to graze his cows, and Pattu bolted and barred the door and sat behind it with a stout cudgel.

At five o'clock in the afternoon, Krishna, who knew all this through his divine insight, went to Kittu's house, assuming the exact form of Kittu and with cows exactly like his and knocked at the door. Pattu opened the door and let him and the cows in. 'Has that wretch been here?' asked the supposed Kittu. 'No. I have been waiting here all day to break his head to bits if he came. Go in and take your meal. You must be tired!' said Pattu. 'All right, Ma. Take care that the blackguard doesn't sneak in. He may assume any shape, you know, and he has got such charming and deceptive ways. We honest husbands are uninteresting. We toil and moil and give our wives nice food to eat and fine clothes to wear. But the ungrateful ones treat us like muck and store up their strength and beauty for these gallants who play and dance and go about seducing other people's wives.' 'Don't worry, son. Go and make merry with your wife. I shall be here and shall tackle that rogue when he comes.' The supposed Kittu then went in and had his meal and spent his time talking to Sundari in exactly as uninteresting a fashion as her husband and she saw no difference.

At six o'clock the real Kittu returned with his cows and knocked at the door. Pattu opened it and at once concluded that the ever-resourceful Krishna was playing this trick on her. Triumphantly, she raised her stick and dealt blow after blow on Kittu, shouting, 'Rogue, I have caught you at last. No more shall you go gallivanting after other people's wives assuming the forms of the real husbands.' 'Ma,' said Kittu, 'I am your son Kittu, why do you beat me?' 'My son!' said Pattu delivering further blows. 'My son Kittu is inside, happily talking to Sundari whom you wanted to seduce. A lucky thing he came before you!' 'He must be Krishna,' said Kittu amazed. 'Ma, don't you recognize these cows, our cows?' 'They are in too! They came with him. So you have brought a duplicate set of cows too!' and Pattu rained more blows. 'Mother, can't you identify my voice? I am the real Kittu. That man inside is a fraud,' said Kittu. 'I know all your tricks. What! Have you assumed my poor Kittu's voice too!' and she rained more blows. 'Oh, let me at least go away alive. I don't want my wife or mother,' said Kittu. 'You shall not get away so lightly,' answered Pattu. 'It is no joke philandering about in honest people's homes and seducing young girls who don't know how to add up even two and two,' and she rained more blows on him. 'Oh Krishna! Oh helper of the distressed, come to my rescue! You are my best friend, and not this hag whom I loved and trusted as my mother,' prayed Kittu. 'You call me a hag, do you?' said Pattu, and gave him some more blows.

Hearing the loud cries of Kittu, Krishna and Sundari went to the door. 'Son,' said Pattu to the supposed Kittu, 'the wretch has been caught and is being given a severe thrashing; come, you too give him some blows. He called your mother a hag.' 'Krishna, helper of the poor, save me. I shall never more be so jealous and foolish,' implored Kittu. Then Krishna resumed him real form and said to Pattu, 'Leave him. He is the real Kittu. I simply wanted to rid him of this demon of jealousy. I am only the Universal Husband as I am the Universal Father, Mother, Brother, Sister, Son and Daughter. A woman's love for me no more interferes with her love for her husband than a son's love for me interferes with his love for his father. It only deepens and enobles the other love. Foolish are they who want to own their wives' body, mind and soul. Let them realize that God has his share in every being, in everything; that without Him everything is nought, and that nothing can bold or bar Him out. Kittu,' said he, 'take this gem of a woman and treat her as she deserves.' Kittu prostrated himself before the Lord who embraced him and freed him from all his pains at once. 'He called me a hag, my son called me a hag,' railed Pattu. 'He only opened the door of truth to you a little,' said the Lord, 'forget it,' and He embraced her too, giving her peace and happiness. Then He embraced Sundari too, saying 'My dear, your husband's eyes are opened. Be forever happy.' He then departed, leaving all three delighted.

None but the Brave

Kausika was a great sage, very proud of his habit of always speaking out the truth whether the matter was great or small and whether the result was good or bad. so very proud was he of this doubtful virtue that he styled himself Kausika Satyavadin or Kausika, the Speaker of Truth. One day, when he was doing penance in his forest grove, he saw a traveller fleeing in panic and hiding in a dense bush in the neighbourhood. There were hundreds of bushes all round, and tracking him out would have taken hours.

A dozen robbers also came to the spot in ten minutes, aimlessly searching for the man everywhere; up the trees, and in the pits, and along the footpaths. Then they saw Kausika Satyavadin and knew him at once. 'Reverend Sir,' said the robber chief to Kausika, 'Did you see a traveller go this way? If so, where did he hide? You are famous for speaking the truth at all costs. Speak!' Kausika Satyavadin thought, 'If I speak the truth, these cruel men will kill the poor fellow. But, why should I utter a lie and sacrifice the principles of a lifetime for his sake?' And he told the robber chief, 'There he is, in that bush.' The robbers pulled the traveller out, killed him despite the sage's entreaties, and took away all he had.

When Kausika died, instead of being sent to Heaven as he had expected, he found himself in Hell. Indignantly he asked Yama, the Keeper of Hell, the Lord of the Dead, 'Why am I here?'

'You have been condemned by Krishna to ten thousand years in Hell for telling the robbers the hiding place of the traveller and letting him be killed,' said Yama.'What!' said Kausika. 'Why should I be condemned for speaking the truth?' 'Don't ask me,' said Yama, 'I only carry out orders. Ask Krishna.'

Kausika sought an interview with Krishna. 'Tell me, Lord,' he said, 'Why am I condemned to ten thousand years in Hell for speaking the truth? Is not Truth God? Should a sage ever deviate from Truth?' 'He should not deviate from Truth,' said Krishna, 'if he is strong enough to prevent injustice. God can always speak the Truth as He is All Powerful and can prevent injustice. Man can speak the Truth only when he can prevent injustice. Else, he must refuse to speak the Truth and take the consequences. Where was the necessity for you to be so truthful about that poor man's hiding place, knowing, as you did, that they would pull him out and kill him, and that you would be powerless to prevent the deed? You should have remained silent and taken the risk of being killed yourself. The robbers might, then, never have found the man at all. For the sake of your vanity, you spoke the truth, and this is the punishment. None but the brave can utter the truth always.' And Kausika was ordered back to Hell.

The Sound Aum

There once lived an ascetic who was reputed to know everything about God. One day, God disguised himself as a Brahmin and in order to test the sage's humility and truth, went to him and asked him, 'Can you teach me all about God?' The ascetic, in his initial confidence, began replying with his mouth wide open, and the letter 'a' (as if to say 'Ah! what doubt is there?') came out. But, even as he opened his mouth, a doubt crossed his mind as to whether he could tell the Brahmin all about God. So, the open mouth closed again a little, producing the sound 'u'. In an instant, the doubt increased still more, and the mouth closed altogether, producing the sound 'm' in the process. The ascetic had thus produced in quick succession the three sounds A U M which blended together into the mystic syllable *Aum*. Struck by the solemn sound of *Aum*, and paralysed by his increasing doubt regarding his own ability to teach the Brahmin anything about God, he remained silent and ashamed.

God was pleased by his humility and love of truth, so He revealed Himself, and said, 'Do not be ashamed. Your silence is pleasing to me. Hereafter, the word "Muni" shall mean "a great sage". But, wise men like you need not remain silent from fear of error. They may communicate to earnest inquirers whatever they think is true, prefixing everything with the mystic syllable "Aum" which you have just uttered.'

From that day onwards, in India, the syllable *Aum* has been adopted as the initial mystic word used before teaching anything about God or indeed anything at all, as there is no subject wholly unconnected with God. It means 'What I am going to tell you is only very imperfect, and may not stand the ultimate test, and it may even be better if I remained silent like that wise Muni who first uttered it. I break this silence only because God has directed us to communicate to all who desire to know whatever they sincerely consider to be the truth.'

Warriors of Old

Just before the Mahabharata War, Krishna and Arjuna were taking a walk by the side of the Yamuna. Arjuna was getting very proud of his archery. He asked Krishna why Rama should have taken so much pains to construct a land-bridge to Ceylon when a bridge of arrows could have quite easily taken all his troops across. 'Perhaps,' he added, 'Rama was not, after all, so great an archer. I could have easily managed to transport all the men with a bridge of arrows.' 'The soldiers of Rama were enormous in size,' said Sri Krishna.

'What if they were?' asked Arjuna.

'Well, then,' said Sri Krishna intending to teach Arjuna a lesson. 'There is just one soldier of Rama still left. You construct a bridge of arrows and transport him at least across this river Yamuna.'

'How ridiculously easy!' said Arjuna, and soon constructed a bridge of arrows across the river. Sri Krishna called Hanuman and asked him to cross the river by the bridge. Hanuman shrugged his shoulders. 'Arjuna, Hanuman perhaps thinks that the bridge is not strong enough. Please see whether your bridge is perfect,' said Sri Krishna.

'Perfect,' replied Arjuna. 'It is the unfamiliarity of it that causes this doubt in Hanuman.'

'Hanuman, cross the bridge without fear,' ordered Sri Krishna. Hanuman placed one foot on the bridge of arrows which came tumbling down into the river with a crash. The monkey jumped back to the shore in disgust.

Arjuna threw down his mighty bow and arrows and declared that, after such a disgrace, he was unfit to fight again.

'Don't be dejected, Arjuna,' said Krishna. 'Even Rama could not do it. What wonder then if you failed? Come, pick up your bow and arrows and hereafter don't try to belittle the famous warriors of old.'

Got Into the Nostrils

Bhima was very proud of his muscular strength. He believed that none could excel him in all the three worlds.

One day, Krishna took all the Pandava brothers and Draupadi to Heaven for sight-seeing, leaving Bhima to come by himself, since he had nothing to fear from the gatekeepers, owing to his known ability to defeat them. Krishna took all the five in, and both the gatekeepers kept quiet on seeing Him. When the party had seen everything worth seeing in Heaven, Drauapadi reminded Krishna that Bhima had not still arrived. 'Perhaps, he has already killed the poor gatekeepers,' suggested Krishna. Coming outside, they found the gatekeepers sleeping at their post, and poor Bhima with his club getting sucked into the nostrils of one or the other of them at every inspiration of theirs and being pushed out again at each expiration; the gatekeepers were not so much as aware of his presence there. Poor Bhima looked a miserable sight.

Krishna saw that he has been sufficiently humbled, took pity on him, woke up the gatekeepers, and released him from his agony.

Gargi and the Brahmagnani

Gargi, the celebrated lady philosopher of ancient India, was wandering about in her usual quest for greater knowledge. One day, she heard of a real Brahmagnani dwelling in a remote forest. Eager to profit from his conversation, she made a weary journey to that distant forest and sent word through one of the disciples of the Brahmagnani for permission to see the great teacher. The disciple returned saying that his master was a sanyasi and would see no woman. 'I see,' said Gargi, smiling, 'Now, I do not want to meet him.' The disciple went back and told his teacher what Gargi had said. The holy man was wonderstruck and was curious to know why she, who had come such a long way to see him, was so little disappointed at his refusal. He ran after Gargi and asked, 'Why, O Gargi, why do you say that you don't want to meet me now; you who have come such a long way with no other object?'

'Sir,' said Gargi, 'I was wrongly informed that you were a real Brahmagnani and so was anxious to see you, in spite of all difficulties. Now that I know that you are no real Brahmagnani, my desire to talk to you is gone.' 'How dare you say, O Gargi, that I am no real Brahmagnani?' asked the sanyasi angrily. 'Because,' replied Gargi, 'a man who really knows Brahma would have made no sex distinctions which you did.'

Winner Yields the Prize

Janaka, the famous king of Mithila, once called an assembly of five hundred philosophers and offered gift of one thousand of the finest milch cows to the greatest amongst them all. Thereupon the sage Yagnavalkya asked his disciples to drive the cows home. No one dared to contest his right. The philosophers said among themselves, 'Oh, what a good thing it would be if we could get the thousand cows or at least two for each of us! But we may as well hope to shake the Himalayas as he shakes Yagnavalkya in argument and wins the cows.' Then out stepped Gargi. 'Venerable sirs,' said she, 'is there not one amongst you clever enough to challenge Yagnavalkya's claim? It is a shame to yield the cows to him without a fight.' None of the learned men replied. 'Gargi,' said Yagnavalkya, 'there is no one here who will dare to argue with me.' 'Well then, when men hang back, a woman must rush in and fight. As the king of Kasi or the prince of Mithila faces a superior enemy, certain of defeat but ashamed to yield without a fight, I am now facing you with two sharp, pointed questions.' 'Ask them, O Gargi.' 'What lies between the earth below and the sky above? Are they separated by vacant space, or ether which is united and mixed with God, the Absolute.' 'At the command of the Absolute, Gargi, the sun and the moon stand in their places; whole worlds are born and whole worlds are dissolved. Though the Absolute cannot be seen, He sees all. Though He cannot be heard, He hears everything.

Though He is beyond sense perceptions, He regulates the senses of every one. Though He is beyond intellectual comprehension, He is omniscient. He created this world and the stars, the sun and the moon and all the things that are in this universe.'

'And who created Him?' asked Gargi.

'Nobody created Him. He created the whole universe out of himself as the spider does the web. But He is the Eternal Verity, the one without beginning or end, the unborn, the uncreated, the ancient. He always was, is, and will be.'

'Now, my second question.' said Gargi. 'Will all the riches of the world secure God and immortality?' 'Oh, no,' said Yagnavalkya, 'By wealth you can only enjoy life as long as you live, but you cannot get immortality.' 'Then, why not give us all two cows each?' asked Gargi. 'I shall give them with all my heart,' said Yagnavalkya. 'Friends choose two each for yourselves. My disciple will drive the last two home.'

The Greedy Brahmin

Somadatta was a Brahmin of little learning but had great presumption. He was also lazy by temperament though he wanted all possible comforts. He lived in Vaisali.

Mahavira, the great Jain prophet, lived in the same town. At the age of thirty, Mahavira gave away in charity everything he had, plucked his hair by the roots with his own hands, to show his utter abnegation of all love of flesh, and became a sanyasi. As he had given away everything including his clothes, the God Indra presented him with a divine robe to wear. Just when Mahavira had put it on, Somadatta went to him and begged for something. 'I came late. I got nothing. You have given to hundreds. Give me something also,' said Somadatta. As he had nothing else to give, Mahavira cut Indra's robe in two and gave one half to Somadatta. The Brahmin was pleased for the time being and rushed off with it. He showed it with pride to a weaver friend of his. He said, 'This robe is really a marvellous one, but it is not long enough. What can you do with half a robe? Now, if you had the other half too, you will have a robe worth having. Go and ask Mahavira for the other half also.' Even Somadatta was ashamed to go and beg for the other half, but his cupidity was roused.

He went and watched Mahavira stealthily. Mahavira was doing penance in a prickly pear bush oblivious of everything around him, and the half robe had, like all half robes, slipped off and fallen on the thorns. Somadatta stealthily crept up to him after making sure that he was in such deep meditation that he would not notice anything, and took the coveted half robe after a dozen thorns had run into his hand and caused profuse bleeding. He went away with it. Mahavira woke up from his meditation just as he was going away, but said to himself, 'Oh, this wretched property which I still clung to made that man a thief,' and resolved to go naked thereafter.

Somadatta sold the cloth to a noble and soon spent the proceeds in eating and drinking with his concubine, who was in the family way. When it was all exhausted, his mistress said to him, 'In a month our baby will be born. At least two gold pieces will be required for the delivery expenses, and a gold piece per month will be required for the baby's keep.' 'But I have nothing at all,' said Somadatta, 'What shall I do?' 'The king of Sripural, Srivardhana, gives ten gold pieces to the first Brahmin he sets his eyes on every morning. Go to him and get them.' Somadatta thought it was a sound idea.

He went to Sripura, made enquiries and found the information given by his mistress to be true. In his excessive greed to obtain the ten gold pieces, and fear that other Brahmins might be seen by the king earlier, he went at midnight into the palace so that he might be the first Brahmin seen in the morning. The sentries, seeing a stranger enter the palace grounds at midnight, took him for a thief, arrested him and produced him before the king. He said to the king that he was no thief but an honest Brahmin and that he had gone to the palace in order that he might be the first Brahmin seen by the king in the morning and secure the ten gold pieces that he so badly wanted for his mistress's delivery. He told his whole story. The king was pleased with his honesty and said, 'Ask for anything within my power and you shall get it.'

Somadatta's greed was roused. He said, 'I shall think it over and tell Your Majesty.' He sat in a corner of the palace and thought and thought over it. He at first wanted to ask for ten gold pieces, then it rose to twenty, hundred, thousand, hundred thousand, a million, ten millions. Still, his greed kept on rising.

Just then, Mahavira, who had gone on a visit to the king and was sitting in the palace grounds, was discoursing to a disciple. Somadatta heard, 'Greed and anger are insatiable demons. The more they are fed, the more they grow. The wise man who desires peace plucks them up by the roots as our monks do their hair.' Somadatta was converted. 'What a slave I have become to greed!' said he and forthwith abandoned all idea of asking for any favours, plucked his hair by the roots, and got initiated as a monk by Mahavira.

Anger Destroys

One day two ascetics were doing penance in Kunala village. That year, as luck would have it, there was no rain in that village though there was good rainfall in all the surrounding villages. Some farmers one day said to one another in the presence of these two ascetics, 'It is the penance of these men which has withheld rains in our village. Else, the clouds, which are always hovering over us, would have burst here instead of migrating to the neighbouring villages.' The ascetics heard this and were terribly angry. Said one ascetic, 'Oh clouds, rain in torrents.' 'And rain for fifteen days and nights continuously,' said the other. Because of their spiritual powers, the clouds obeyed. It rained in bucketfuls in Kunala, night and day, for fifteen days continuously. There was a flood sixty feet deep, and all the buildings collapsed, and all living things perished, including the farmers and the two angry ascetics.

The Last Chain Broken

Indrabhuti was the greatest disciple of Mahavira. He and his ten brothers had been Brahmins given to sacrificing animals but had been convinced by Mahavira's gentle teachings and had become his chief disciples along with Sudharma, another Brahmin, the son of Dhamila and Bhaddila. Indrabhuti soon mastered Mahavira's teachings thoroughly but could not yet become a kevali as he could not get rid of his attachment to his master. Mahavira saw this and said to him, 'Oh, Indrabhuti, to be born as a human being is extremely precious as it is only a human being who can, by his efforts, get rid of past karma and free himself from the chain of births and deaths. Especially is this so when one is born an Arya like you. You have crossed the great ocean, then why do you halt so near the shore? Make haste to get on the other side and reach the world of perfection where there is safety and perfect happiness. Be not attached to anything. Shake off your intense attachment to me. It is the last remnant of possessiveness and egoism. Rid yourself of it.' All was in vain. Indrabhuti tried and tried, but his love for his great master always prevailed and brought him to his side whenever he was ill or in danger.

Finally, the great Mahavira lay dying at Papa. He had that day expressly sent Indrabhuti on an errand to Kundagrama, a village some miles away, and had once more impressed on him the necessity to sever himself from his intense attachment to his

master. 'This body of mine will soon be lifeless matter' said he.
'Before it becomes that, Oh, Indrabhuti, exert your will and get
rid of your attachment, and become a kevali.' Indrabhuti left for
Kundagrama in a thoughtful mood.

The king of Papa, Hastipala, was a follower of Mahavira.
Mahavira sat in the king's Hall of Great Authors and delivered
his last sermons to the king and his other disciples. At the end,
a messenger entered and said, 'Oh Exalted One, Indrabhuti has
returned and is standing outside the city walls, unsettled and
walking to and fro like a man wrestling with a great problem.'
After ten minutes another messenger entered. Mahavira asked,
'What is Indrabhuti doing now?' 'He is standing outside the gate
plunged in deep mediatation.' After another ten minutes, a third
messenger entered. Mahavira asked him, 'What is Indrabhuti
doing now?' 'He is going back to Kundagrama, Oh Jina,' replied
the messenger. 'That is good,' said Mahavira, 'It shows that
he has severed his attachment for me and has finally got rid of
possessiveness and egoism and become a kevali.' Then, retiring
inside, the great teacher plunged into deep samadhi and died all
alone, and severed the chain of birth, old age and death. News of
this reached all the surrounding towns and villages. Indrabhuti
heard of it and came and saw the corpse of the master whom he
no longer loved. 'Since the light of intelligence is gone, let us
make an illumination of material matter,' said he, and organized
a feast of lamps, the origin of the Jain Dewali festival, and had
the corpse burnt.

The Muslim Governer Won Over

Chaitanya, the famous Vaishnava saint of Bengal, began his bhajanas and sankirtanas. He invited all people irrespective of caste or creed to join him. He attacked the mere learning of the Pandits as so much dead weight unlivened by the spark of faith. 'Teach the message of Krishna,' said he, 'from the Brahmin to the outcaste.' The Brahmins and Pandits were angry at this and at the equality conceded to the lowest of the low. They could not oppose Chaitanya by themselves as they were but a handful of selfish men and the mass of the Hindus was for him. They foresaw the sure loss of all their privileges and false prestige if the great democratic devotional movement of the saint was allowed to triumph. In their desperation, they sought the help of the Muslim rulers, forgetting that they were the enemies of Hindu religion of all denominations, including theirs. They told the Muslim governor that Chaitanya was preaching the idol worship of Krishna to all people including Muslims, and that it was the governor's duty to stop this. The governor knew the character of the traders and the motives which had moved them to complain. He had also heard of the purity and devotion of the saint. Still, he, as a Muslim governor, was expected to do as they had indicated. So he forbade all bhajana parties in the town, and had the instruments of one of Chaitanya's followers who disobeyed the order broken to bits. Chaitanya forthwith organized three bhajana parties. At the head of the biggest party he went to the governor's own house. The governor, who had heard credible accounts of the saint's purity and holiness, did not want to arrest him as he would be bound to do if he witnessed his open disobedience of orders. So, he shut himself up in his house, fastening every door and window. But Chaitanya called out to him to open the door and receive him like a true Muslim. 'The Prophet has said, "Whosoever believeth in one God and in a future life, let him honour his guest. It is one of my ways that the host should come out with his guest to the door of his house." How can you disobey his precepts?' asked he. So the governor opened the door and came out and received him. Chaitanya then asked him. 'Why did you direct the instruments of my friend to be broken when he was using them in praying to God? Has not the Prophet said, "He whom prayer preventeth not from wrong-doing and evil, increaseth in nought, save in remoteness from the Lord." 'Yes, but can God be adored with music like that?' asked the governor. 'Has not the Prophet said, "Adore God as you would if you saw Him, for if you see Him not, He seeth you?" People receive you with music. Won't you do as much to God?' 'But your own people asked me to break the instruments and prohibit these bhajanas,' said the governor, 'Has not the Prophet said, "That person is not of us who calleth others to aid him in oppression?"' asked Chaitanya. 'But they are learned men too,' remonstrated the governor as a last excuse. 'Has not the Prophet said, "The worst of men is a bad learned man?" asked Chaitanya. The governor was convinced. He said, 'Brother, you seem to know much more of our religion than I do. Do what you like. Carry on your bhajanas and kirtanas, and reap the consequent reward or punishment.' Thereafter he and Chaitanya had the greatest regard for each other.

Charity

King Yudhistira was very proud of his charity in feeding 16,008 Brahmins every day from the magic all-providing pot which he had. All these Brahmins used to follow him whereever he went and eat the sumptuous meals given to them free. Sri Krishna wanted to humble Yudhistira's pride. So one day, he took him to the underworld where the righteous King Mahabali ruled. Mahabali received Lord Krishna with all proper worship. The latter then introduced Yudhistira to Mahabali, as his cousin. At once Mahabali went and most respectfully invited Yudhistira to his kingdom.

'Ah!' said Sri Krishna to Mahabali, 'you don't know the full extent of the goodness of my cousin, who is the abode of charity. He feeds 16,008 Brahmins gratis three times every day, and they follow him wherever he goes.'

'Pooh!' said Mahabali, spitting on the ground. 'What a wretch he must be to keep 16,008 people so helplessly dependent on him simply to satisfy his vanity! Even if I offer a kingdom, no man will come shamelessly to me three times every day for meals. Oh, Lord, is this cousin of yours the abode of charity, the Model King of whom I have heard so much?' Yudhistira was humbled to the dust at this well-merited reproach.

Reckless of Life

Chaitanya used to teach his disciples, 'If you want to see God you must be reckless of life. You must not fear being drowned or burnt or killed or starved to death. Once this life is dedicated to Him, it is no longer yours. It is for Him to preserve or destroy it. So, store not and fear not!' He and his disciples used to be content with whatever was offered by the pious that day. They never stored up anything. One day, in a Muslim village, they did not get the sacred myrobalan used for putting on the ceremonial caste marks. One of the young novices said to Chaitanya, 'Sir, I have got one.' 'Who brought it?' asked Chaitanya. 'Nobody here brought it. This is a Muslim village. We cannot get it here. Knowing it, I saved up a myrobalan yesterday from what they gave in the Hindu village and have brought it here.' 'Son,' said Chaitanya, 'have I not asked you not to accumulate and make plans or lay stores for the future? You are more fit to be a householder than a sanyasi. Leave me, marry and settle down.' The novice burst into tears and begged to be excused and retained. 'I cannot retain you as you have broken our rules. But, don't grieve. You can meet me whenever you want. Marry and work out your acquisitive instinct and, then, become a sanyasi.' The young man was consoled and left.

Some days later, Chaitanya was in Nuddea with his disciples. Two notorious brigands, Jagannath and Madhava, nicknamed Jagai and Madhai, lived there. They were Brahmins by caste but were confirmed meat-eaters and drunkards. They were exceedingly cruel at heart and had robbed thousands. Two of Chaitanya's disciples, Nityananda and Haridas, went to reform them and convert them. They found them rolling in the dust of the road in front of their house with a big mud pot of liquor, nearly empty, near them. They asked them to say Govinda, and leave off drink, robbery and other vices; to say Hari and turn over a new leaf! The drunkards got up in wrath. Jagai hurled the pot on Nityananda's head where it crashed and broke to pieces, causing blood to flow down his cheeks freely. Madhai beat Haridas savagely. Nityananda and Haridas fell down unconscious. Some spectators went and told Chaitanya about these incidents and requested him to rush to the aid of his disciples after taking the help of the Muslim governor. Chaitanya said, 'I shall go there at once. But I need no help.' He went to the spot, sending word to the brigands in advance that he was coming alone and without taking any aid from the Muslim governor or others, and that they might get all their mud pots and sticks ready. Jagai and Madhai wondered at the courage of this saint. When they saw him come, his fair form, loving eyes and fearless gaze stirred in them feelings of remorse and repentance. Jagai, however, asked Chaitanya, 'Why don't you avoid us, seeing that we may even kill you?' 'I am reckless of life,' said Chaitanya, 'when I am doing my duty. Krishna owns this body, not I. It is for him to keep it or destroy it. Did you expect a devotee of Krishna to fear you, you wicked men? Krishna can tackle a million of you without an effort. Do you think he will not take you to task for attacking his devotees?' Nityananda, who had recovered consciousness by then, said to Chaitanya, 'Forgive them. I am not suffering at all.' Haridas said, 'It is drink which made them beat me. Forgive them.' The robbers fell at the feet of Chaitanya and said, 'Punish us as you think fit. Even death at your hands will be a great honour for us. Born in a respectable family of Brahmins, we have sunk in oceans of liquor and committed all the sins known to man. What medicine can there be for us?' 'There is a supreme panacea for all human ills. Say Govinda! there is enough salvation with him to go round. When lightning flashes, the darkest night becomes the clearest day,' said Chaitanya. Then he raised and embraced them. The brigands left their vices and became his fervent disciples.

During Chaitanya's wanderings, a Brahmin leper called Vasudev went to see him. Even the outcasts used to flee from Vasudev owing to repulsion at the sight and stench of his leprosy and the fear of catching it. Vasudev said from a distance, 'Govinda! Govinda!' and shook with emotion at the sight of the Master. Chaitanya went to him and embraced him. 'Oh God,' said Vasudev, 'I am a miserable leper. Even outcasts shrink from me. And your gracious self has embraced me and blessed me.' 'The devotee of Krishna should fear nothing,' said Chaitanya. 'Brother, your physical leprosy is nothing. You have the spiritual striving which will get you to Heaven. It is the moral lepers who must beware.'

When Chaitanya was going from Puri to Brindaban, he fell into a trance and a few passers-by at once rushed to his aid and held him. Some Pathan soldiers who were passing by just then mistook those helpers for robbers and bound them hand and foot. When Chaitanya recovered from his trance, he told the soldiers that these unfortunate men deserved rewards rather than ropes. Then he discoursed with them and a Muslim religious man about God and things divine and converted them all. 'It is a capital offence to convert Muslims,' said a man to him, 'so, leave them alone.' 'One life may be lost by converting them. How many lives will be lost by not converting them?' asked Chaitanya. 'Say Govinda and rid yourself of fear.' All said 'Govinda! Govinda!' and the Muslim converts were then known as Pathan Vaishnavas.

Once, in a forest, Chaitanya defeated a Buddhist monk in all his arguments. The monk and his followers, infuriated at the defeat, treacherously offered him poisoned rice pretending that it had been offered to Govinda. When Chaitanya was about to take it, one of his followers said to him, 'Master, these men appear to be unreliable. Touch not this food.' 'What nonsense!' said Chaitanya. 'The worst poison will be destroyed by uttering the name of Govinda. Say Govinda and eat it.' All cried out 'Govinda! Govinda!' Just as Chaitanya was about to eat the rice, the Buddhist, who had been impressed by his faith, fell at his feet and said, 'Sir, pardon us. Touch not this rice. It is poisoned,' and took it away and destroyed it and brought fresh rice, and all ate it together, crying out 'Govinda! Govinda!' From that day, all those Buddhists became Chaitanya's followers.

When he was forty-eight, Chaitanya's religious ecstasies became very intense. Once, uttering devotional songs, he walked into the ocean to see Narayana of the living waters, and was pulled back by his disciples with great effort. Again, he hit his head against the stone pillars of the Jagannath temple to see God face-to-face, saying, 'You appeared before the demon Hiranya when he struck a pillar. Won't you appear before your devotee?' He went on with bhajana parties, dancing and singing, reckless of the night and darkness and the uneven nature of the ground. A brick pierced the saint's toe and caused a septic wound of which he died. He was asked when dying, 'Oh, Blessed One, why were you so reckless of life?' 'The tank is intended to catch the water, the body to realize the Lord. A tank without water and a body in which the Lord does not dwell both exist in vain. So, my disciples, be reckless of life. Teach devotion to Krishna from the Brahmin to the Chandal. Be free from the six passions and reck not what happens to you. Cling not to fleeting life, but to the giver of life everlasting, Govinda!' said he, and died.

Bailing Out the Ocean

The great Pundarika heard that Vishnu, as Narayana of the moving waters, was sleeping away in the sea of milk his cosmic sleep of preservation. This sea of milk is represented by the milky way in the sky and by the Palk Straits on the earth. Being desirous of seeing God face-to-face, and unable to search the Milky Way, Pundarika went to Palk Straits. At dawn he bathed, said his prayers and began to bail out the sea water with his copper vessel in order to see Vishnu sleeping underneath. He went on bailing out the water throughout the day, forgetting the hot sun and the quantity of the water in the ocean, and even the fact that the water bailed out by him was going back to the ocean through the sands. Just as the sun was setting, Vishnu disguised himself as a Brahmin, went to Pundarika and said, 'Whatever are you doing?' On Pundarika's telling him, he laughed and said, 'What a fool you are! Can you bail out the water of the ocean with this miserable pot even if you did so for eternity? See the water flowing back to the ocean through the sands. Go home and eat, and desist from this foolish task.' 'Brother,' said Pundarika, 'if you want to help me, take a pot and bail out water with me. Else, go away and leave me to bail out the water alone as before,' and he resumed his bailing, ignoring the Brahmin altogether. God then resumed His form and showed Himself to Pundarika, and said, 'Faith such as thine can move mountains, dry up the ocean, improvise a ladder to the heavens. Such devotees are specially dear to me.'

Snakes Settle the Creed

Cheraman Perumal, the Emperor of Kerala, was converted to Islam by a celebrated Arab missionary. He asked all his nobles and subjects also to become Muslims. They were quite unwilling to do so. Finally, they all agreed to abide by an ordeal suggested by the high priest, a very clever Brahmin. The Arab missionary and the high priest were each to take and put a snake in a mud pot and seal it up. The opponent was to break the pot and challenge the snake, in the name of his God, to do its worst. He who emerged unharmed was to be the victor. If the Muslim priest won, all the nobles and subjects were to become Muslims. If the Brahmin won, they were to remain Hindus, and Cheraman was to go into voluntary exile to Mecca after partitioning his kingdom into three parts, Malabar, Cochin and Travancore, among three great nobles.

The momentous day of the ordeal arrived. The Brahmin and Muslim went out to a grove infested with snakes. The Brahmin took a five-foot cobra in the very presence of the Arab, put it into a mud pot, and sealed it up. The Arab, who knew nothing of India or its snakes, wanted to select a longer snake, and chose a six-foot rat snake in the sight of the Brahmin, put it into a mud pot, and sealed it up. Then they went to the great assembly with their sealed pots. Under the king's orders they exchanged the pots.

The Brahmin priest, knowing the harmlessness of the contents of his pot, broke the pot without fear and cried out,

'Oh snake, in the name of Brahma, I challenge you to do your worst!' The released rat snake slunk away in terror. The Arab was anxious to show that he feared the contents of his pot even less. With gusto, he too broke his pot and cried out, 'Oh snake, in the name of Allah, I challenge you to do your worst.' The cobra, thus released, raised its hood in terrible anger and bit the Arab priest who soon died of the poison. The nobles and people of Kerala remained Hindus. Cheraman Perumal partitioned his kingdom into three parts, giving Malabar to the Zamorin, and Cochin and Travancore to the respective Rajas, and went into voluntary exile to Mecca. The cobra thus saved Hinduism in Malabar, and became more sacred than ever.

Swallower Swallowed

Lopamudra was the only daughter of the King of Berar. She was entrancingly beautiful, and had the sweetest and most winsome nature on earth. When she came of marriageable age, the sage Agastya went and asked for her hand in marriage. The king and queen was most unwilling to give their beautiful daughter to this poverty stricken sage, but were afraid of his curse should they refuse. Lopamudra knew the sage's worth and so went and told her parents, 'Grieve not for me. Bestow me on him.' Her parents then decked her in the costliest robes and jewels and gave her in marriage to Agastya.

After the marriage, Agastya said to her, 'Throw away those costly robes and jewels and put on a homely saree and follow me. A poor man's wife should be dressed accordingly.' Without a second's hesitation, Lopamudra did as he desired.

Agastya went to the banks of the Ganges and did his penance. Lopamudra attended on him most lovingly. When the penance was over, Agastya wanted to live with Lopamudra and have a son. Lopamudra said, 'Beloved, I want you to give me costly robes and ornaments as I had in my father's house.'

Agastya then went to King Srutarvana, considered to be very rich, and asked for some wealth. Srutarvana showed him his accounts and convinced him that his income and expenditure were the same and that he himself could do with some wealth. So, they both went to King Vradnaswa reputed to be still richer. He too had nothing to spare. Then the three of them went to King

Trasadasya reputed to be still richer. Even his accounts showed no surplus, and Agastya never wanted to take that which might be required by others. So the four of them went to the demon brothers Ilvala and Vatapi.

Ilvala was reputed to be rich beyond the dreams of avarice, but the brothers had the evil repute of eating up their guests in a peculiar fashion. Vatapi used to assume the form of a goat and Ilvala used to cook him and serve him and his guests. When the unfortunate guests had partaken of the repast, Ilvala used to call out: 'Vatapi, Vatapi', and Vatapi used to rip open the stomachs of the guests and come out, and the two brothers would then eat up the bodies of their guests with relish. Many a sage and beggar had thus been eaten up by the demons.

The three kings told Agastya about this horrible practice and warned him about approaching the demon brothers. Agastya replied, 'There is enough fire in my belly to digest any demon. Don't you fear. Come along.' They went to Ilvala who received them most hospitably and promised a hundred thousand rupees and robes and gems to each after they had been his guests and eaten his dinner. So Vatapi turned himself into a goat, and Ilvala cooked him. As arranged between the four guests, Agastya ate up the whole of Vatapi. Ilvala was delighted at the folly of the great sage and contemplated with joy the luscious repast they would make of him and his three comrades. After Agastya had eaten the entire meat, Ilvala called out as usual, 'Vatapi! Vatapi!' But, Vatapi did not come out. Agastya belched and said laughing, 'That is the last left of Vatapi, Ilvala, my child. This belly has enough fire in it to digest ten Vatapis.' Ilvala was terror-stricken. He was afraid for his own safety. He paid the four guests a million rupees and countless gems and robes each, and sent them away. Agastya went and gave the gems and robes to Lopamudra and enjoyed a wondrous honeymoon.

The Belly God's Exploits

One day, Siva said to Parvati, 'We are in all the creatures. So, let us take every form by turn and live together.' The goddess agreed. When they were living together as elephants, Parvati conceived a child. She was afraid that she would deliver an elephant cub. She did not like the idea at all. But Siva told her, 'What harm is there?' She insisted that something should be done. At last Siva said, 'Very well. The baby will be born with an elephant's head and a human body. He will be of astounding intelligence and will be the supreme helper of mankind in overcoming their obstacles.' In due course, Ganesa was born. He was a great favourite with gods and men. The great gods Brahma, Vishnu and Siva ordered that anybody worshipping them should first worship him. With his trunk, elephant face, protruding belly and never-failing good humour, he was remarkable even among gods for generosity, wisdom and sound common sense.

He had nothing aristocratic about him. His vehicle was a mouse, and his chief delight lay in eating. His younger brother, Subrahmanya, had a beautiful human head, and very aristocratic ways. His vehicle was a peacock and his weapon the spear.

Subrahmanya thought that he was more intelligent than Ganesa and did not at all see why Ganesa was given the first fruits by all the gods. He complained once to his parents that he was in no way inferior to Ganesa in knowledge and common sense. Siva and Parvati said to him, 'All right. We shall test you.' They called Ganesa and Subrahmanya together and offered a prize to the one who would go round the universe first. Overjoyed at such a test, Subrahmanya at once set out on his peacock and began travelling round the universe, beginning with the Milky Way. It took him seven years of strenuous non-stop flight. Ganesa had simply gone round his father and mother in seven seconds. When the jubilant Subrahmanya returned after seven years and claimed the prize, and sarcastically remarked that he never even met Ganesa on the way, Ganesa laughed and said, 'One extracted the oil. The other turned the empty oil mill a thousand times. You went round an empty universe in seven years. I went round our parents, the living universe, in seven seconds and got the prize. Shall I show it to you?' Subrahmanya bit his lips in disappointment and went and took service as a General under Indra, the king of the gods, where everything was done by red-tape and nothing was sprung on anybody. Ganesa was made the commander of Siva's heavenly hosts.

Time flew. The demon Ravana did the most terrible penance on the Himalayas. This pleased Siva very much, from whom Ravana took a lingam which, as long as it was with him, would make him invincible in any fight. The only reservation was that till it was taken to his land, Lanka, it should not be placed on the ground anywhere as it would take root wherever it was laid.

The gods were dismayed at this great gift to Ravana. They said, 'We must somehow deprive the demon of this lingam before he reaches Lanka. Else, he will destroy all the gods and men.' In despair they approached Ganesa and said, 'You alone can save us.' Ganesa agreed to do so. Taking the form of a Brahmin boy of twelve he followed Ravana. When the latter reached Gokarna, he felt the necessity to pass water. As the lingam could not be kept with him when he was doing such an act and could not also be placed on the ground, he looked out for somebody to hold it till he had finished the act and the necessary ceremonial ablutions. He was delighted to see a Brahmin boy near by. He asked the boy to hold it for him and strictly enjoined him not to put it on the ground. The boy said 'All right. But if you don't come after I have called you thrice, I shall place it on the ground and go away.' Ravana agreed, as he thought that he would be able to take back the lingam in a few minutes and did not suspect any mischief. But, just as he sat down and began to pass water, the boy called out: 'Ravana, Ravana, Ravana' thrice in quick succession, and, before he could rise and go to him, he put the lingam on the ground and ran away. When Ravana went to the spot in a hurry he found the lingam stuck firm. All his efforts to remove it were in vain. The demon was no longer invincible. The gods rejoiced and praised Ganesa and his resourcefulness.

Time again flew on. Siva, in a weak moment of pity for mankind, promised heaven to all men who worshipped his lingam at Somnath. All kinds of fellows, sinners of every denomination, went and worshipped there and so crowded heaven. Indra and the gods were panic-stricken. Heaven was fast becoming an overcrowded suburb with all kinds of nondescripts in it. And more and more of them were arriving every second. 'At this rate, there will be no space for gods and angels,' wailed the gods, 'and hell will be a better and quieter place.' All of them sought Ganesa's aid. He promised to divert the traffic in no time.

Ganesa went and sat near Somnath temple. Thousands of nondescripts eager to enter heaven were coming along to worship the lingam. 'Where are you going, brethren?' asked Ganesa. They told him. 'That is silly,' said he. 'What is the use of a promise of something good for you when you are no longer alive to enjoy it? Worship me and I shall give you, in this world, what you desire.'

Picking out an elderly man, he asked, 'What do you want?' 'A fine house to live in and good food to eat. I have no house and am starving. That is why I want to go to heaven,' said he. Ganesa gave him a splendid mansion and many delicacies every day. He prostrated to the belly god and went away rejoicing. A childless couple wanted children and were promised half a dozen, and returned after breaking coconuts to Ganesa. A boy wanted to pass his examination and was promised not only a pass but a first class. So he promptly gave up his idea of going to heaven and returned to his house and examination. A man with a stomach-ache was given a cure and forthwith returned home. So, all the pilgrims returned home and advised the intending pilgrims to leave Somnath alone and concentrate on Ganesa. Heaven was relieved from the threatened overcrowding, and Ganesa became the most popular of all the Hindu gods.

The Triumph of the Goddesses

Brahma, Vishnu and Siva, the great gods of the Hindu Trinity, once had a consultation together as to the share their consorts, Saraswati, Lakshmi and Parvati who should be allowed in the decisions made by them on cosmic affairs. They finally agreed that their consorts were in no way entitled to consultation on cosmic affairs and were only personal companions to save them from solitude. They duly communicated their decision to the goddesses who, in turn, held a consultation together on Mahalaya Amavasya day and decided on leaving their husbands severely alone till their rights were conceded.

Saraswati, the goddess of learning, left her husband Brahma, the god of truth. The cosmos was plunged in confusion. Nobody respected Brahma any more as he was truth devoid of learning and was classified with the dumb animals. Nor did many respect Saraswati as she was now learning devoid of truth, but still she had a few select followers from among the elite. Brahma held out for nine days and surrendered on the tenth day of the Dasara, Vijayadasami Day, when Saraswati is worshipped and general feasting observed in commemoration of the reunion of Brahma and Saraswati, truth and learning.

Then Lakshmi, the goddess of wealth, began her campaign against her consort, Vishnu, the preserver. She first withdrew the waters of the Sea of Milk on which her lord was reclining. Vishnu was inconvenienced, but thought that he could manage as well on the empty sea bed. But Lakshmi withdrew that too, and Vishnu was poised in mid-air. He resolved to carry on. Lakshmi withdrew the air too and he was in a vacuum. 'What is there to preserve in a vacuum?' asked he in indignation. 'Ah, now you see,' said Lakshmi, 'it is my affairs you manage, and you must therefore consult me.' Vishnu agreed on the morning of the same Vijayadasami Day when Laksmi is worshipped and general feasting is observed in commemoration of the reunion of Vishnu and Lakshmi, happiness and wealth.

Now Parvati, the goddess of the burning ground, began her campaign against her consort, Siva, the god of destruction. She knew the vanity of her lord and so induced a demon, Mahishasura, to get from him a boon that no god or man or demon could defeat him. The demon got the boon and promptly attacked his benefactor, Siva, as demons will do. Siva fled. So did all the other gods. Men and angels implored the gods to do something to stop the ravages of the demon who was eating up a million men every day. None of the gods could do anything. Nor did the other goddesses respond. Saraswati said that learning would not avail against a demon. Lakshmi declared that wealth would not induce a demon to give up eating men and angels. So all went to Parvati and implored her to do something. She said, 'I shall do something if Siva will acknowledge the error of his ways and promise to consult me in everything hereafter.' Vishnu, Brahma and men and angels went to Siva's hiding place and compelled him to agree to her terms for the sake of the universe.

Then Parvati started on her lion and waged war on the demon. 'You are but a demon,' said she, 'and no match for me, a woman.' The demon knew in his heart of hearts that she was right, and lost all hope of victory. Still, he fought on desperately at the head of his hosts. The universe shook as the terrible demon and the more terrible goddess fought on. At last the goddess triumped over the demon and his hosts. Left and right lay millions of dead whom she had killed. Intoxicated with the carnage, she danced about, destroying even the men who came to thank her. None dared to face her. The universe seemed destined to be destroyed in a few hours. 'The demon would have destroyed it in a few years, she will destroy it in a few hours, oh my poor universe,' wailed Brahma the creator. 'Go and save it quick,' said Vishnu to him. 'I can't, I am hiding from the demon, and she is stronger than the demon. How can I face her? You go and stop her. She is your sister,' said Brahma. 'I don't care for the errand,' said Vishnu. 'After all, married sisters don't care so very much for their brothers. Moreover, a husband is the proper person to control his wife. Let us send Siva.' And poor Siva was compelled by all to go and stop his wife from further destruction.

Siva approached her diffidently as she was dancing her dance of destruction. She did not recognise him and tripped him down in the course of her dance, and danced over his chest. The gods, led by Brahma and Vishnu, raised a cry of despair and indignation. 'No Hindu wife has done it before,' said they. Parvati then looked down and saw that she was treading on her husband. Filled with sudden shame, she put out her tongue. Seeing herself naked and unadorned, she cut off the arms of some of the demon troops, strung them together, and wore them round her loins. She cut off the heads of some demons, strung them together with Mahishasura's head in the middle, and wore them round her neck as a necklace. Then she raised her husband and embraced him, and he became one with her as Ardhanariswara—'Half-Man, Half-Woman'. It was Vijayadasami morning then, when Parvati is worshipped and general feasting is observed in commemoration of the reunion of Siva and Parvati, Right and Might.

Prepared to Go to Hell

The great law-giver Manu said that impotent people, reprobates, the born blind and deaf, mad men, idiots, dumb men and people lacking a limb should be held to be unfit to be heirs, but that those who succeeded to the properties to which the former would otherwise have succeeded were bound to give them food and clothing worthy of their position, on pain of falling into the deepest Hell. Till the other day, this was the law applicable to Hindus in British India and even today, some Hindu states follow it.

In one of the states where the law holds good even now, the heir to a rich estate was a man born blind. He had no children. So the whole estate went to his younger brother who was so cruel that he refused to give even food and clothing to his blind elder brother. The blind man complained to the courts. The younger brother appeared in court and said that he was prepared to fall into the deepest Hell, and that that was all the punishment prescribed by Manu for refusing maintenance to such disinherited persons. The judge, however, said that Manu had declared that all people who wilfully chose Hell were reprobates and that in this case he had specifically said that persons who refused to maintain disinherited relatives were 'extreme reprobates', and so, in the end, ordered that the younger brother also should be disinherited and that the estate should go to a cousin who was directed to maintain both the disinherited brothers according to their social status.

Sudama

Sudama was a poor brahmin boy who became a close friend of Krishna in sage Sandipani's hermitage. Krishna learnt to chant from Sudama.

Once, Sandipani's wife asked Sudama and Krishna to get some wood from the forest. While they were collecting the wood, a storm came and they got lost. Sudama was scared. Krishna held his arms and assured his safety. When the storm was over, they found their way to the hermitage. Sudama was relieved. Sandipani blessed them with long life and happiness.

After completing their studies, Sudama and Krishna went their own ways. Krishna became the king of Dwarka and married princess Rukmini, the goddess of prosperity. Sudama, on the other hand, married a simple brahmin girl and began to lead the life of a devotee, reading scriptures, praying, forsaking worldly pleasures. Everyone loved Sudama. His family was quite happy.

Then Sudama's wife gave birth to two children. Because of Sudama's austere lifestyle, the family began to face difficult days, with little food to eat and no clothes to wear. Sudama's wife was extremely devoted to her husband but when her children began to suffer, she was concerned.

Finally, on a cold night, when her children were without a blanket, she approached Sudama and humbly said, 'Aren't you and Krishna, the lord of Dwarka, friends? And, Krishna married to the goddess of prosperity, Rukmini?'

Sudama replied, 'Yes.'

Sudama's wife dreamed of seeing an improvement in her family's poor condition. She earnestly said, 'Go, my lord, I beseech you, for the sake of our dear children, meet Krishna.'

The very prospect of meeting Krishna, his old friend, made Sudama happy. 'I will go and see him, but I will not ask him for anything.' Sudama's wife could hardly conceal her joy. She happily said, 'Even a visit to Krishna will bless our family. Do not ask anything from him. I will be content my lord.'

Just before his departure for Dwarka, Sudama came to his wife. Both had the same thought. 'What will I give to Krishna when I see him after such a long time?'

Sudama's wife suddenly remembered, 'My lord you used to tell me that Krishna immensely loved powa, the flattened rice!' Sudama, too, remembered Krishna's great liking for powa. Sudama's wife ran to her neighbour's house and they happily gave her the gift of powa in a small bundle. Sudama then set out on his long journey to Dwarka.

When Sudama came to the palace, surprisingly enough, no one stopped him.

He looked through various rooms and finally located Krishna and Rukmini. When Krishna saw Sudama he ran to embrace him. Then Krishna sat down and washed Sudama's tired feet with warm water and put sandalwood paste on them.

After the royal meal, they all settled down to chat. Krishna and Sudama exchanged the happenings of their lives since they departed from Sandipani's hermitage. Suddenly Krishna noticed a small bundle tied to Sudama's waist. He remarked, 'Ah! You have brought a present for me!'

Sudama hesitated, 'How do I give a king a poor man's powa?' When Krishna noticed that Sudama was ashamed to give him the bundle, he remarked, 'Sudama, the poorest gifts given to me with love is dearer to me than the richest of gifts given without love.' Krishna was thoughtful, 'He has not come to ask anything for himself. He came out of love for his wife and me.' Then he quickly snatched off the bundle and opened it. There it was, his favorite powa! He tossed some in his mouth with great satisfaction. Then they talked and talked, as old friends, to their heart's content. Sudama could not ask anything from Krishna.

Next morning Sudama bid Krishna and Rukmini farewell. The long road back home did not seem to be that hard as he thought of Krishna. When he reached home, he was amazed to see that a huge mansion was standing in place of his poor hut. His wife and children, wearing new clothes, came to receive him. He could hardly recognize them. Sudama felt the touch of the all-knowing Krishna, who had rewarded Sudama for his gift of love.

Sudama continued to lead the life of a hermit while his family enjoyed the generous gifts of wealth from Krishna.

Narada and the Sun and the Moon

The sun and the moon had a dispute one day as to which of them was greater and more useful to the world. Naturally, as in all such disputes between two people, they could not come to any agreement. So, they went to the divine sage Narada, whose wisdom and tact were famous even in Heaven, and asked him to give his verdict. 'The sun is greater during the day and the moon during the night,' said Narada. The sun was more or less satisfied, but not so the moon, which was cocksure of success if a definite verdict was given. 'Don't equivocate. Tell us definitely who is absolutely the greater all the time,' said the moon to Narada. 'Don't press me, it is not good for you,' said Narada. But the moon would not listen. 'It is best to know the truth once for all,' said the moon. 'Be it so,' replied Narada. 'Then, I shall ask you alternately to go into hiding for one day so that I may judge which of you is greater and more useful to the world.' 'All right,' said the moon, delighted and sure of success, and went into hiding first on full moon day in order to make its success doubly sure. The world had only the sun's light that day. All people missed the usual brilliant moonlight and cursed the sun for the stupid quarrel which had caused them this loss. The moon was delighted. It told Narada, 'Do you hear those curses? Is there any doubt in your mind now as to who is greater?' 'Wait till tomorrow is also over,' said the sage. Next day, the sun hid, and the world was plunged in darkness during the day. All work was at a standstill. People cursed the wretched moon for its silly quarrel with the sun and said, 'Now, we shall have to work in the night with the aid of the moonlight which is a poor substitute for sunlight.' But night came, and there was no moonlight even though the moon was right overhead. There was pitch darkness everywhere. The moon asked Narada, 'Why is there no light in me, oh sage?'

'Because,' said Narada smiling, 'yours is a reflected light borrowed from the sun. The sun being now in hiding, you cannot shine in borrowed splendour. Now you know who is greater all the time.'

Bhrigu and Brahma

The other sages were a little put off by Sri Krishna's saying in the *Bhagavad Gita* that of all great sages, the greatest was Bhrigu. They asked Krishna to prove to them that Bhrigu was superior to them. So Krishna assembled all the sages except Bhrigu and asked them to plunge in deep meditation, closing their eyes. When some time had elapsed, Krishna called out, 'Oh, ye sages, Brahma is coming.'

All the sages at once opened their eyes, and asked Krishna 'Where is He? Where is He? We don't see Him.'

'He is gone,' said Krishna. 'Let us see whether He will go to Bhrigu.' Then they all went to Bhrigu who was plunged in deep meditation in his Ashram.

'Bhrigu,' said Krishna, 'Brahma is coming.' Bhrigu paid no heed. His eyes were closed as before.

'Bhrigu, Brahma is coming,' said Krishna again in a louder voice. Bhrigu neither opened his eyes nor spoke.

'Bhrigu, don't you hear?' said Krishna a third time in a still louder tone. 'Brahma is coming. Don't you want to see and worship Him?'

'Which fool is it that speaketh to me?' asked Bhrigu, still with his eyes closed. 'Is not Brahma within me, am I not seeing and worshipping Him always? How can He, who never was absent, come? Every sage looks for God within himself and not without.'

'Do you see the reason why I preferred Bhrigu to you?' asked Krishna of the other sages.

How the Sun Became Less Fierce

One night Aruna, the goddess of dawn and the mother of Surya the sun god, woke up from her sleep, sweating and agitated. A voice had whispered to her that if she didn't take care, her son would leave her and wander away to some distant horizon. If that happened, the universe would forever be plunged in darkness.

In the morning, Surya was feeling restless. He felt he must set out on a long journey. So he announced to his mother that he was going out for a ride through the sky. Aruna hid her fear. Instead she flashed him a broad smile and said, 'Surya, my son, what a lovely idea! I think I will come with you. Would you like me to be your charioteer?'

Surya was very fond of his mother. Besides, he knew she was very good with horses. So he agreed, even though he had been looking forward to riding on his own.

Surya's chariot was drawn by seven horses, each with gleaming coats like brownish-red silk and adorned with tassels of gold. He climbed into the chariot and Aruna hoisted herself into the charioteer's seat.

She flicked the whip and the horses began to trot. Soon they were galloping through the skies. As the wind rushed through his hair, Surya felt a tremendous sense of exhilaration. 'Mother, I don't feel so restless any more,' he screamed, and Aruna smiled back, saying, 'I know! I know!'

As they rode along, Aruna spotted a beautiful young girl in a garden full of flowers. She was singing and frolicking with her maids. Suddenly Aruna had an idea. She steered the chariot close to the garden and, just as she had hoped, she saw Surya and the girl look at each other.

Surya was not very tall but he had a body that was muscular and shone like burnished copper. When he smiled, its radiance melted even the hardest of hearts. Now he smiled at the girl, and she, enchanted by him, blushed shyly.

'Who is that?' Surya asked aloud.

'Sanjana,' Aruna said. 'Her father is Vishwakarma, the architect of the gods.'

'What a beautiful girl,' Surya said. She will make someone a wonderful wife? Aruna stopped the chariot and asked him, 'Would you like to marry her?'

Thus Surya and Sanjana's marriage was arranged. When the ceremony was over, Surya led his bride to his palace, and that was when their troubles began. Until then they hadn't been together, and now when Surya went to sit next to Sanjana, the heat of his radiance scorched her skin. It singed her flesh and burnt her insides. Sanjana couldn't stand the heat and she fainted. When Sanjana was roused by her maids flicking water on her face, she began to weep, 'I cannot stay with him. His radiance will burn me to ashes.'

Her maids helped her escape and, in her place, she left Chhaya or shade. Then, taking on the form of a mare, Sanjana fled to a dark forest. There she wandered stricken with sorrow and guilt. She loved her husband but if he came close to her, she knew she would die. When Surya discovered that his wife had left the palace, he went in search of her. Soon he found Sanjana and, unwilling to be separated from her, he changed himself into a stallion and went towards her. Sanjana was overjoyed to meet her husband in a form that was both pleasing and splendid. 'We shall never be separated again,' they said to each other.

But both Aruna and Vishwakarma were worried. The universe was in darkness. How could there be life without Surya spreading his light? 'What can we do?' Aruna asked, 'Surya will not consent to take his original form if it displeases Sanjana and poor Sanjana will be burnt to ashes even if he does.'

Vishwakarma thought for a while and said, 'There is only one thing to be done. I will have to chisel away some of his brilliant rays so that Sanjana and he can live together as husband and wife.'

So Vishwakarma went to the forest in which Surya and Sanjana now lived and cut away one-eighth of Surya's rays. The fiery trimmings fell to the earth. Two of them became Vishnu's disc and Siva's trident. And since Surya had lost some of his radiance, it was possible for Sanjana to be with him. So they took their real forms and went back to live in their palace.

Vishnu's First Avatar— The Matsya

Once upon a time there lived a good and holy man called Manu. But Manu was not happy because everyone around him, including his wife and children, were dishonest and wicked people. They laughed at his honest ways and taunted him for being a silly fool. But Manu refused to be swayed by their words and went about life in a quiet and righteous fashion.

Sometimes though, he would become very sad and desperate and then he would fold his hands in prayer and beseech the gods, 'When will you take me away from these evil people? Is there to be no end to my suffering?'

Every morning, just before he sat down to eat his breakfast, Manu would fetch a small pot of water from the well to wash his hands. One morning, as he poured water over his hands, he heard a tiny voice cry, 'Help! Help!'

Surprised, Manu looked around him and into the well. But he could see no one. Then he looked into the pot of water and in it was a tiny horned fish. As Manu watched, the fish opened its mouth and spoke to him in human voice, 'Preserve me and I will preserve you!'

Manu smiled and said, 'Don't worry, I shall not harm you. But how will you help me? You are so tiny that a frog can swallow you in one gulp.'

The fish swam a full circle and said, 'I cannot reveal the

future to you but preserve me and I shall preserve you…'

So Manu left the fish in the little pot and put it away in a safe place. He knew if his children saw the fish, they would kill it just for fun. Every day Manu fed the fish and it talked to him about life and the importance of being a good human being. The fish grew rapidly and soon he had to move into a tank at the bottom of his garden. But the fish continued to grow and so he moved it to a nearby lake. But it wouldn't stop growing and Manu turned to the fish for help, 'You will soon be bigger than the lake…Where shall I keep you now?'

'Take me to the ocean and come to see me every day. Soon it will be time for me to fulfil the purpose for which I was sent here,' the fish said and Manu did as it asked him to.

The ocean was a few hours away from his house. After the fish moved to the ocean, Manu would go there every evening with a bag of puffed rice. When he scattered the rice on the waves, the fish would appear before him.

One evening, it was waiting for Manu and when he walked into the waves, the fish said, 'Manu, the time has come for you to plan your escape. I want you to build a ship and keep in it the seed of every living being. You too must live in it. Do not stay in your house once the ship is ready.'

Manu was bemused by the fish's orders. But he trusted the fish greatly. By now Manu had realized that it was no ordinary creature. So he went to the forest and set about chopping some sturdy trees. As he built his ship, his family and neighbours mocked him.

'Ho, ho, ho, going somewhere, are you?' one man said.

'What a fool he is! He's building a ship so far away from the sea. How do you plan to get it into the water? Will you wait for the rains to sweep it away? Ha, ha, ha…' his family laughed.

But Manu went about his task. Soon the ship was built and he began to live in it.

'He has gone mad!' his wife shrieked. 'Why has he stopped living in his house and started living in a ship that's not even in the sea?'

But Manu refused to get angry and continued to live in the ship. Every evening he went to meet the fish, which had grown as big as a hill now 'Tonight's the night,' the fish said. 'There will be a great storm and the flood waters will destroy all living creatures. Stay in your ship and I shall come for you.'

Manu rushed home to warn his family and the whole town. 'Come into my ship. You will be safe there. The flood waters will kill all of you,' he cried. But no one would listen to him.

That night, a great storm blew. It was a storm so powerful that no one had seen anything like it before. Rain poured down in torrents, lightning flashed continuously, and the waters of the ocean rose higher and higher. Soon the whole world was submerged. No man, woman or child survived, except Manu, who stayed dry and warm in his ship that floated on the surface of the rising water.

The fish arrived when the storm was at its peak. 'Manu,' it said, 'fasten a cable from the ship to my horn.'

Manu did as the fish asked and it towed his ship through the waters. They sailed high above the Himalayan peaks and the tall mountains of the world. The journey took many days and years and Manu began to feel lonely. He missed human company. 'Is the world to end with me?' he worried. 'Am I to be the last man on earth? Please, gods, help me. I would like to have some children, to love and protect and to leave the legacy of life.'

So Manu was granted a wife, and when the flood receded, they went back to live on the earth. Their children became the ancestors of mankind.

As for the fish—Matsya—it was none other than Vishnu, the preserver of the universe.

Vishnu's Second Avatar— The Kurma

In the deluge, some of the rarest things in the world were swept under the waters. Much of that which was precious and irreplaceable was washed away. The gods decided to try and retrieve them. But they knew it would be an impossible feat unless they had help. So a delegation of gods went to the asuras to ask for their assistance. The asuras agreed to help, for they too desired some of the rare treasures, especially amrita, the nectar of life, which would make them immortal.

It was time to begin the search. But how would they reach into the vast depths of the ocean where the precious things now lay? 'We should churn the ocean, for only then will the rare objects float to the surface,' Brahma said.

So the gods asked the great serpent Vasuki to let them use its strong coils as the rope. The mountain Mandara would be the churn. Varuna, the lord of night and the oceans, was asked to hold the mountain steady so that the churning could begin.

But he found the mountain much too heavy for him and had to give up. He fell on the ground, sweat running down his brow and chest. 'I can't do this,' he gasped, too tired to even speak. The gods now needed to find someone else to hold it.

Vishnu's anxiety for the churning to start was greater than anyone else's for he knew that his consort Lakshmi was hidden somewhere in the cosmic ocean. Since a base was required to fix the mountain to the ocean bed, Vishnu offered to help. He took the form of Kurma—a giant tortoise—and his back, the tortoise shell, became the pivot for the mountain.

The serpent Vasuki was twisted around the mountain. The gods took hold of the serpent's head, and the asuras grabbed the tail end. Together they set about churning in. And with it both good and bad began to emerge from the deep waters. The great tugging and pulling of the serpent against the mountain caused it to exhale heavily and his breath emerged as a thick mist. The clouds burst into rain and fell on the gods, who welcomed the showers. However, when the snake started spouting poison, many died. The movement of the mountain killed many animals in the sea. But the rubbing serpent against the mountain squeezed the juices from the medicinal plants on its slopes. These juices ran down the slopes into the sea, which revived these creatures. The rubbing also set off many fires, and Indra, the lord of lightning, had to make the rains come again to put out the fires.

Then, as the gods and the asuras continued with the churning, from the waters emerged the wondrous things which had been lost. First emerged Kamadhenu, the cow of plenty. It was given to Vashishta, the officiating priest. Then came Airavata, the stately white elephant, and Uchchaih-sravas, a wonderful horse, which were both claimed by Indra. Then emerged Sura, the goddess of wine, and following her from the whirlpool sprang the Parijata tree, which Indra said would be kept in heaven so that all celestial beings might enjoy its delicate fragrance. Then came Rambha, and the other celestial nymphs who later became dancers in Indra's court; next came the moon, which Siva seized and wore as a hair ornament.

The gods and the asuras churned the ocean for a thousand years and still there was no sight of the nectar which was what they were really seeking. Instead, what came up was visha or poison. The snake gods drank as much of the poison as they could, but there was still so much left that it looked as if it would strike them all dead with its flames. To prevent this, Siva drank up all the poison, which lodged in his throat, turning his neck blue in colour. Now with renewed vigour, the churning began again. Shankha, the conch of victory, emerged, as did Kaustubha, a priceless jewel. Finally from amidst the froth, Lakshmi rose, with a lotus in her hand. Along with her, the ocean yielded the much-prized water of life. Wearing white robes, the god of medicines, Dhanwantri, appeared, bearing the jar of amrita in his palm.

The churning finally came to an end and the asuras now discovered that almost everything had been claimed for their own by the gods. This angered them so much that they snatched the pot of amrita and a battle started.

Siva decided to intervene and said, 'Since both the gods and the asuras have worked equally hard to churn the ocean, I suggest that the nectar too be divided equally.'

'But who will divide the amrita?' everyone asked.

At that moment a beautiful woman appeared. Nobody had seen such loveliness before and all were dazzled. She said her name was Mohini. She smiled at them and said, 'Allow me to divide the water of life.'

Both the gods and the asuras agreed.

'Since the gods are elder to the asuras, they must be served first,' she said. The asuras were so enchanted by her that they agreed to that as well.

Everyone sat down in two rows with their plates in front of them. Mohini started serving the gods first, and since there were thirty-three of them, all that was left after they had been served were a few drops, which she poured down her own throat.

Just then the moon and the sun, who knew Mohini was actually Vishnu, spotted that Rahu, an asura who had disguised himself as a god, was sitting with them and had been served a portion of the amrita. They told Vishnu, who promptly hurled his sudarshan chakra at Rahu and cut off his throat. But the nectar had already slid down his throat, so his head and body remained alive separately. The head was called Rahu and the body, Ketu. Since then Rahu wreaks revenge on the moon and the sun by occasionally swallowing them up and plunging the world into darkness. But he cannot hold them for long and they always reappear. We call this an eclipse.

When the asuras realized that Vishnu had tricked them to ensure that only the gods became immortal, they were furious Another battle started. But the asuras were tired after the churning and the gods were stronger than ever after having consumed the amrita. And so the asuras were defeated once again.

Vishnu's Third Avatar—The Varaha

Hiranyaksha and Hiranyakashipu were asura twins. They were groomed to be the chiefs of the asuras when they grew up. Even as children, they hated the gods and promised themselves that they would defeat them when they grew up.

One day Hiranyaksha, the older twin, had an idea. 'It is the people on the earth who give these gods delusions of grandeur. If there was no earth, then who would remain to pray to these gods,' he thought.

No sooner than he realized this than Hiranyaksha set off to destroy the earth.

He dragged the earth to the bottom of the ocean and stood there holding it close to his chest.

'What shall we do now?' said one of the gods as they all gathered together. 'All those millions of people, birds, animals, trees, and flowers everything is at the bottom of the ocean. How can we bring it all back?'

'Even if we go to the ocean bed, how can we take on Hiranyaksha? He is stronger than all of us put together,' said another god. Vishnu decided to fight Hiranyaksha. He assumed the form of Varaha, a gigantic boar, and swam to the bottom of the ocean. He challenged Hiranyaksha, and the ensuing battle continued for a thousand years.

Finally Vishnu slew the asura. Picking up the earth with his horns, he tossed it back to the surface. As soon as the earth was restored to its place, the birds sang as they did at the crack of dawn, the animals shook themselves awake from their long sleep, the leaves began to rustle and even the spider that had paused for more than a thousand years began to weave its web. And the people went about their lives as they used to. All was well again.

Fourth Avatar—Narasimha

When Hiranyakashipu discovered that his twin had been killed by Vishnu, he decided to obtain a boon that would make him indestructible so that a similar fate would not befall him. To achieve this, he began a long penance to appease Siva.

When Siva finally appeared before him and offered him a boon, Hiranyakashipu asked that he should be made invincible.

'Even though you have proved your devotion to me, that I cannot promise,' Siva said.

'In that case, I would like you to give me a boon that will ensure I cannot be destroyed either by man or animal, neither indoors nor outdoors, neither at day nor by poison or weapon,' Hiranyakashipu said.

Siva looked at him carefully, then smiled and said, 'So be it!'

Hiranyakashipu was certain that no one could defeat him now. The king of the asuras began his wars against the gods. He went to battle with Indra and wrested heaven away from him. There he began to dwell and rule heaven, the earth and the netherworld as if he were its only lord.

The gods went pleading to Siva, who was in deep meditation, to help them. Siva opened his eyes and said, 'You will have to endure your suffering for some more time. Hiranyakashipu's end is drawing near.'

The king of the asuras had a son named Prahalada.

Hiranyakashipu was very fond of his son but his fondness turned to irritation when he discovered that his son was an ardent devotee of Vishnu. 'Who is this Vishnu fellow?' he bellowed. 'There is only one lord in this universe and that is I, your father, Hiranyakashipu. If you wish to worship someone, then repeat after me, "Om namo Hiranyakashipu!"'

But Prahlada refused to say such a prayer and continued with his prayers to Vishnu.

Hiranyakashipu watched his son's devotion and grew angrier and angrier. 'He is not my son,' he thundered. 'He is a traitor. Like all traitors, he deserves to die.'

Hiranyakashipu ordered that a rogue elephant be brought and made to trample the boy. But when the elephant saw Prahlada and heard him mutter, 'Narayana, Narayana,' it fell to its knees and dropped a garland of wild flowers around the boy's neck.

Angered by this failure, Hiranyakashipu let loose poisonous snakes on the boy's bed when he was fast asleep. But the snakes merely stood guard around the boy. When Prahlada woke up, they went away without harming him.

But the king was not ready to give up. He lit a pyre and had Prahlada thrown into it. Prahlada stood with his eyes closed, his hands folded in prayer, and continued to say, 'Narayana! Narayana!' Suddenly, a huge thunderstorm arrived out of the clear skies and sheets of rain put out the flames.

Furious, Hiranyakashipu dragged his son to the palace. 'Who is this Narayana? Where does he live?' he asked the boy.

'Narayana lives everywhere,' the boy said.

'Does he live here?' the asura demanded, slamming a door. 'Or does he live here?' he said, pushing down a table. 'Or is he crouched inside this pillar?' he asked, smashing the pillar with his mace.

The pillar fell apart and from it emerged a strange-looking creature. It was Narasimha, half man and half lion. It had the head and claws of a lion and the body of a man.

When Prahlada saw the apparition, he recognized instantly that the half man-half lion was Vishnu. He fell on the ground and exclaimed joyously, 'Oh, my lord, you are finally here!'

As the assembled courtiers watched in amazement, Narasimha grabbed Hiranyakashipu and dragged him towards the door of the palace. He paused on the threshold. For there it was neither indoors nor outdoors. Then, with his claws, that were neither weapon nor poison, and at twilight, which was neither day nor night, he ripped open Hiranyakashipu's stomach and pulled his intestines out.

Thus did Vishnu kill the tyrant Hiranyakashipu, but without breaking any of Siva's promises.

Prahlada became the king of the asuras, returned heaven to Indra and made his subjects happy till his death.

Vishnu's Fourth Avatar—Narasimha

When Hiranyakashipu discovered that his twin had been killed by Vishnu, he decided to obtain a boon that would make him indestructible so that a similar fate would not befall him.To achieve this, he began a long penance to appease Siva.

When Siva finally appeared before him and offered him a boon, Hiranyakashipu asked that he should be made invincible.

'Even though you have proved your devotion to me, that I cannot promise,' Siva said.

'In that case, I would like you to give me a boon that will ensure I cannot be destroyed either by man or animal, neither indoors nor outdoors, neither at day nor by poison or weapon,' Hiranyakashipu said.

Siva looked at him carefully, then smiled and said, 'So be it!'

Hiranyakashipu was certain that no one could defeat him now. The king of the asuras began his wars against the gods. He went to battle with Indra and wrested heaven away from him. There he began to dwell and rule heaven, the earth and the netherworld as if he were its only lord.

The gods went pleading to Siva, who was in deep meditation, to help them. Siva opened his eyes and said, 'You will have to endure your suffering for some more time. Hiranyakashipu's end is drawing near.'

The king of the asuras had a son named Prahalada.

diminutive and it was as a little man he went to King Bali's court asking for alms.

King Bali received Vamana as though he were a very important guest and asked, 'What can I do for you? How can I be of service to you?'

Vamana looked up at the king and said, 'All I need is three feet of land!' 'Is that all?' Bali asked in surprise. 'Don't you need anything more?' 'Three feet of land will do,' Vamana said.

'Then it shall be yours. Do take it from wherever you want,' the king said, amused by the little man's modest request.

Then, as the king watched, Vamana began to grow rapidly. He multiplied in size until he was as tall as the trees, as tall as the mountains and finally as tall as the skies. With his left foot, Vamana covered the earth. 'This is the first foot of land,' he said, his voice ringing through the skies. With his right foot, he covered heaven. 'This is the second foot. What is left, O king? Where shall I take my third foot of land from?'

King Bali realized that this was none other than Vishnu and that the third foot of land had to be found. So he fell on his knees and bent his head, 'All I have left is my head. Take this as the third foot of land,' he said with quiet dignity.

When the gods saw this, even they were moved to tears by Bali's humility and honour and rained flowers on Bali. But Vamana put his foot on the king's head and pressed him down into the netherworld. 'Henceforth, this shall be your kingdom,' he told King Bali.

As Bali was about to leave the earth for good, his grief-stricken subjects gathered to bid him farewell, When the king saw the tears in his people's eyes, he too was saddened. 'How can I stay away from my subjects?' he thought.

Bali turned to Vamana and said, 'I have one request before I leave. All I ask is that for one day in the year I be allowed to visit my people and know all is well with them.' Vamana agreed.

Ever since, the king's subjects wait for his coming year after year. To this day, the people of Kerala welcome King Bali with a carpet of flowers every year. This day is known as Onam.

How the King Became Vishwamitra

King Gadhinandana went deep into a forest on the slopes of a mountain and there, by the side of a stream, he performed rigorous austerities. He meditated for a thousand years and achieved such a perfect state of concentration that Siva appeared before him and wanted to know why he was subjecting himself to such pains.

'I want to be Vashishta's equal. I want to have an army that matches his. I would like to possess and be able to use the Brahma-astra,' Gadhinandana said.

Siva granted him these wishes.

The king summoned the army of fearless warriors bequeathed to him by Siva and rushed to Vashishta's hermitage. 'I shall show the sage who is stronger,' he said to himself.

As the vast army drew closer, the inmates of the ashram began to fear what was to happen to them. 'Do not worry,' Vashishta said. 'Go about your duties. No harm shall come to any of you.'

When the king's archers began to shoot arrows at the hermitage, the arrows fell to the ground, bent and twisted. It was as if the hermitage was cloaked in a metal armour. The king and his men tried their best but to no avail.

Finally, Gadhinandana brought out the Brahma-astra, the deadliest of weapons which would find its target and raze it to ashes. But when he hurled it at the ashram, it had no effect.

Defeated, the king stood at the door of the hermitage and cried, 'Sage, tell me what makes you more powerful than me.'

Vashishta laughed. 'You are a warrior and will always remain one. So you seek blessings to destroy me. But I will not blame you for that. You are destined to behave that way.'

'I do not agree,' the king retorted. 'Our birth cannot decide how we behave. I shall prove to you that I too can be a Brahma rishi just like you.'

The king retired to the forest and began another thousand years of penance. Brahma appeared before the king and said, 'You have proved yourself. Henceforth, you shall be called Vishwamitra.'

The king looked pleased but he was still not satisfied. 'What kind of rishi am I?' he asked.

'You shall be a raja rishi, a kingly sage,' Brahma said.

'But I want to be a Brahma rishi. I want to be Vashishta's equal,' the king cried.

'You will be a raja rishi,' Brahma said and disappeared.

The king who was now known as Vishwamitra couldn't get Vashishta out of his mind. He began to look for ways to prove that he was Vashishta's equal or even superior.

How Bali Was Defeated

Kiskindhya was a kingdom in the southern part of India. It was ruled by Bali, the monkey-king, whose father was Indra, the king of gods. When Bali was very young, his father was so pleased by his conduct that he gave him a boon. Indra blessed his son that no matter who battled with Bali, the opponent's powers would be reduced by half and the powers would shift to Bali during the time of the battle.

Soon no one could vanquish Bali and he became so very powerful that he defeated Ravana in a wrestling combat.

Once a demon, Dundupi, approached Bali and challenged him to a duel. Furious at the demon's effrontery, Bali decided to teach him a lesson. He began to wrestle with Dundupi. But the demon managed to free himself from Bali's clutches. But Bali would not let him go; he chased the demon into a cave. He stood at the mouth of the cave and called to Sugriva, his younger brother, 'I am going after the demon and when I get him in my hands, I will break every bone in his body. I want you to wait here till I come back. If milk flows out, you will know that I have succeeded. But if blood flows out, you must leave immediately and protect our families and kinsmen.'

Sugriva waited outside the mouth of the cave. Some time later he heard Bali yelling, 'Help! Help! I'm being killed!' Then, to Sugriva's horror, he saw a rivulet of blood flow out of the cave and knew that his brother had been vanquished. In anger and grief, he rolled a mighty rock and sealed the mouth of the cave. Then he went back to the kingdom and assumed the role of the king.

However, what had really happened was that the demon had realized he was about to die and in his final moments had played a trick. As he struggled, he called out in a voice like Bali's and, when he saw Bali invoke a rivulet of milk, he conjured it to look like blood. Bali was unaware of the trick and set about beating the life out of Dundupi. After Bali killed the demon, he came to the mouth of the cave and found a huge rock blocking his way. He stared at the rock in surprise and then pushed it aside. 'Where are you, Sugriva, my dear brother?' he called. But Sugriva wasn't there. Bali began to get anxious. He rushed to his palace and there he found his brother seated on the throne.

Bali thought his brother Sugriva had wanted to kill him and had sealed the mouth of the cave to ensure that. He stared at his brother angrily, 'So this is what you wanted...all this while you were pretending to be a loving brother and in your head you were plotting my downfall. You are a traitor!'

When Sugriva saw his brother alive and well, he rushed towards him joyously. 'I am so happy to see you. We all thought you were dead!'

'Stop pretending, Sugriva,' Bali roared. 'You mean you thought I was dead! You wanted me dead so you could be king. But you shall no longer be king!'

Sugriva tried to explain. 'I never wanted to be king. But the ministers forced me to be one till your son was old enough to be the ruler. Please believe me, my dear brother.'

'Don't call me brother. If you truly were one, you would have waited for me till I returned,' Bali said.

'But I heard you scream that you were being killed and then I saw blood flow out,' Sugriva said.

'Did you think a demon was going to destroy me?' Bali demanded.

And even though all his ministers tried to explain, Bali wouldn't listen. He banished Sugriva from the kingdom and Sugriva went to the forest with a band of his faithful followers, which included Hanuman, the son of Vayu.

Later, when Rama and Lakshmana passed through the forests seeking Sita, they met Sugriva who told them the sad story of his banishment. He narrated how Bali had seized the throne back and, to make matters worse, had married Sugriva's wife, thereby depriving him of his home and family.

'Everything I have is yours. But I have nothing to offer you,' Sugriva told Rama.

'Do not lose heart. I shall ensure that you get justice,' Rama said.

'But no one can defeat Bali. He is so powerful,' Sugriva said. 'Besides, our father's boon ensures that in a battle his opponent's powers will be reduced by half.'

'Listen to me. I have a plan. This will not be a battle in the conventional sense,' Rama said.

So Sugriva went to the palace doors and roared, 'Bali, come out! I challenge you to a battle!'

Bali looked up from what he was doing and wondered: 'What is wrong with that fool, Sugriva? Has he gone mad? Does he think he can defeat me?'

'Go away!' Bali screamed.

But Sugriva continued to shout challenges. 'Are you so scared that you are hiding behind the skirts of the women in the palace? Perhaps you too should begin to wear one!' he taunted.

Bali lost his temper and stepped out of the palace and they began to wrestle. Rama, who was hiding behind a tree, shot an arrow which pierced Bali's heart and killed him.

Thus Sugriva became king again and his monkey-army helped Rama in his battle against Ravana.

How Balarama Destroyed Two
Mighty Asuras

Once again when the universe was ravaged by evil rakshasas, and there was no one who could vanquish them, the time came for Vishnu to make his appearance. He took two hairs, one black and one white, and set them afloat. These became the children of Devaki. The dark one was Krishna and the fair one, Balarama. As soon as they were born, they were carried away to Gokula so that their uncle Kansa wouldn't kill them.

King Kansa had deposed his father, Ugrasena, as the ruler of Mathura. One day, he was told that his nephews would destroy him and so he murdered each one of Devaki's children. However, both Balarama and Krishna were smuggled away to Gokula soon after they were born, where Rohini looked after Balarama and Yashodhara, Krishna.

Krishna and Balarama were completely unlike each other not only in looks but in their behaviour too. But that didn't stop them from being the best of friends and together they had many adventures.

Just as Krishna killed many demons, Balarama, too, had his share of victories. When Balarama was a young boy, an asura tried to carry him off. The asura had disguised himself as a cowherd and so for a while Balarama sat on his shoulders quite happily. 'Where are we going, uncle?' he asked.

'Your father wanted me to take you to see the new calf which was born yesterday,' the asura said.

Balarama began to feel something was not quite right. He was familiar with every cow and calf in the place and knew that no calf had been born the day before. But he kept quiet. Soon he saw that the asura was walking in the wrong direction from where the cows grazed and he asked, 'Where are you going? This is not the way.'

The asura laughed. 'This is the right way. The way to your death.' But Balarama was not going to give up without a fight.

So he began to beat the demon's head. His hands were so strong that his blows cracked the demon's head and he fell to the ground dead.

Some days later, as Balarama was crossing a narrow bridge, at the other end stood an ass, which refused to budge. It was the great demon Dhenuka in disguise, and his plan was to kick Balarama to death. 'He is a little boy and one kick will be enough,' the demon thought.

Balarama looked at the ass that was blocking his path and said politely, 'I have come all this way. All you need to do is to step a few feet back. Please let me pass.'

Again and again, Balarama appealed to the ass. But the ass brayed and refused to move. So Balarama slapped it on its rump to make it run away. The ass rolled its eyes, snorted and raised its leg to kick Balarama. But the boy was very nimble on his feet and jumped out of the way in time.

Balarama, unlike Krishna, had a quick temper and he lost it now. He also realized that the ass was no ordinary animal. So Balarama seized the ass and began whirling it around by one of its legs till the creature was dead and then he flung the carcass. It landed on a tree and the disguise fell off. Now everyone knew that Balarama had killed the wicked demon Dhenuka.

What Happened When Balarama Wielded the Plough

When Balarama was a young man, he accompanied Krishna to Mathura and helped him destroy Kansa, their wicked uncle. Away from the simple life of Gokula, both Krishna and Balarama discovered the pleasures of royal living. Balarama developed a fondness for wine and sometimes went on drinking bouts.

Once when Balarama had drunk several glasses of wine, he decided to have a bath. After the attendants prepared the bath, he refused to bathe in the palace and said he would like to bathe in the waters of the Yamuna.

'But, Your Highness, the river is far away and you are in no condition to walk or ride to the riverbank,' the attendants said bewildered.

Balarama lolled back on the cushions and said, 'Why should I go to the river? The river will come here. All I need to do is call it.'

The attendants tried to hide their smiles.' He is so drunk that he doesn't know what he is saying,' they thought. Balarama saw their smiles and snorted. 'You don't believe me, is that it? Just watch. Yamuna, hey you river, come to me. I would like to bathe in your waters,' he said loudly.

But the river didn't appear. Balarama called again but the river didn't heed his command. Balarama began to get angry. 'How dare you be so...so...' Balarama spluttered in rage, unable to find words.

He then rose from his seat, grabbed the plough that was his favourite weapon, and stalked to the riverbank. He plunged the plough into the waters and dragged it this way and that. 'You wouldn't come to me. Now you have to go everywhere that I want, you understand?' he muttered.

Balarama walked first to the east, then to the south, then to the north and to the west and then again to the north. All the while he held his plough in the water and the river was dragged after him.

The river began to feel dizzy with the constant change in direction. Yamuna assumed a human form and appeared before Balarama, begging for forgiveness. His pride satisfied, Balarama let it go.

There were many times that Balarama wielded his plough to deadly effect. When Duryodhana, the Kaurava prince, kidnapped and imprisoned Balarama's nephew Samba, and kept him as a prisoner, Balarama asked for his release. Duryodhana laughed scornfully and refused. Balarama thrust his plough under the ramparts of Hastinapura and began to shake it. The city trembled and seemed in imminent danger of collapsing, so finally Duryodhana was forced to release Samba.

Dwivida, a demon in the form of a great ape, longed to get his hands on Balarama's plough. With the plough he would be invincible, he thought. So he stole the plough and began to taunt Balarama. 'Let us see how strong you are without your plough.'

Balarama grunted in reply and grabbed the great ape and began whirling it in the air till blood spewed from its eyes, nostrils, ears and mouth. Then he hurled it on to the ground. The ape fell on the crest of a mountain and such was the weight of its body and the force of the throw that the mountain splintered into a hundred pieces.

Meanwhile, King Raivata, who had a very beautiful daughter called Revati, was looking for a husband for her. Since she was as strong as she was beautiful, he thought he would have to consult with Brahma on who would be worthy of her. Brahma suggested that he choose Balarama and so King Raivata went to Balarama and gave him Revati as his wife.

Balarama looked at Revati carefully. 'She is very beautiful,' he said, 'but she is much too tall and I don't want my wife to be taller than I am.'

So he shortened her with the end of his plough and then married her. Revati might thus have lost a few inches but she didn't lose her incredible stamina. When she discovered Balarama's fondness for wine, she began to join him in his drinking bouts. That way he didn't get drunk and, since she had a strong head, she was not affected, no matter how much she drank. They lived very happily together and had two sons.

How Krishna Taught Indra a Lesson

The people of Vraja, near Mathura, lived off the land. They grazed the cows on the grass that grew abundantly and bathed the cattle in the waters of the Yamuna. The cows produced so much milk and of such wonderful quality that their milk, curd and butter were much sought after. To thank Indra for giving the region plenty of rain, the people of Vraja offered a grand yagna to him year after year.

One year, when Krishna was a young lad, he questioned the elders of the community 'Why do you offer prayers to Indra? It isn't as if he's doing anything extraordinary. It is his business to provide rain.'

'Don't speak like that, Krishna,' they cautioned. 'If Indra gets angry, he'll trouble us with too little rain or too much. Besides, conducting a sacrifice is a tradition. Everyone here has a good time.'

'I'm not saying that we shouldn't conduct a sacrifice. All I'm saying is why do it in honour of Indra?' Krishna said.

'Then who shall we do it for?' the older men asked.

'How about the mountain Govardhan? Don't our cows graze on its slopes? Don't we collect firewood from its trees? Don't we drink the water from its streams? Don't we live on its sides? And have we ever thought of saying thanks to the mountain that is part of our lives in so many ways?' Krishna spoke with a smile.

When Krishna smiled and spoke so sweetly, no one could resist him. That year the sacrifice was conducted in honour of the great mountain Govardhan.

Indra was furious when he found out that the people of Vraja had offered a sacrifice to the mountain instead of him. 'How dare they?' he fumed. 'I'll teach them such a lesson that they will come begging to me and will never dare risk my displeasure.'

So Indra sent a storm towards Vraja and for many days the rain came pouring down. Lightning criss-crossed the skies and thunder rumbled ominously, making cows low and babies cry and old people take shelter under their beds. Everything was sodden and the level of the river began to rise. Soon it had risen beyond the banks and still the rains didn't stop. 'Let me see what Krishna and his mountain-friend can do to save them,' Indra laughed.

Krishna realized that Indra was punishing the villagers.This angered him and he decided to teach Indra a lesson.' Come with me,' he said to the villagers. 'I will take you all a place where you will be dry and safe. Indra won't be able to harm you with his rains or thunderbolts.'

Krishna led them to the foot of the mountain Govardhan and asked the mountain for permission to move it. When the mountain agreed, Krishna lifted it with his little finger and all the villagers huddled together beneath it.

For seven days, Krishna held the mountain aloft. Finally, Indra knew there was nothing more to be done. He went to Krishna and offered his homage. 'Forgive me for my pride,' he said. 'I shall never harm these people again.'

Krishna put back the mountain and the people returned to their homes. From then on, every year, both the mountain and Indra were venerated.

How the Kauravas Were Born

Gandhari was the daughter of Subala, the king of Gandhara. She was to be married to Dhritarashtra, the king of Hastinapura. She was a good woman, kind and generous.

At the wedding, Gandhari discovered that her husband had been born blind. Gandhari decided that she didn't want to see a world that had been denied to her husband. So she wore a blindfold over her eyes for the rest of her life.

One night Gandhari had a dream that she would give birth to a son who would almost entirely destroy the human race. She woke up shuddering, telling herself that it was only a dream. Soon she forgot about it.

A few weeks later, the sage Vyasa visited the palace and Gandhari, instead of letting the attendants take care of the sage's needs, did everything herself, from cooking his food to getting his bath ready, to washing his clothes, to pressing his feet to organising the ingredients for his daily sacrifice. Vyasa was so pleased by her devotion that he asked her, 'What would you like?'

Gandhari bent her head and said, 'I did not expect anything in return.'

'I know that,' the sage said. 'Nevertheless you must have a desire.'

Then Gandhari remembered her dream and said, 'I would like to be the mother of a hundred sons!'

So Vyasa blessed her, 'You shall be the mother of a hundred sons.'

Soon, Gandhari was pregnant. Unlike other women who had their babies in nine months, Gandhari continued to be pregnant for two years. Finally, she delivered a lump of flesh. 'What am I to do with this?' Gandhari asked herself in despair.

Just then the sage Vyasa appeared, and taking the shapeless mass of flesh, he divided it into a hundred and one pieces. One by one, he placed each piece in a jar.

In nine months, in one of the jars, a baby appeared. As soon as he was formed, jackals howled, donkeys brayed, the day became night and a wailing wind rattled the rooftops.

'This child will destroy the world,' everyone said, terrified. 'Leave him in the forest where the beasts will destroy him.'

But Dhritarashtra refused, and brought his son home. The child was named Duryodhana, or the one hard to conquer. A month later, ninety-nine other princes came forth. From the last jar was born Gandhari's only daughter, Dushala, for Vyasa believed every woman ought to have a daughter.

Thus were born Gandhari's hundred sons who were called the Kauravas.

How Agni Got His Strength Back

Agni, the god of fire, was born from a lotus created by Brahma. His complexion was a brilliant red to match the vigour with which he leapt and flickered. Moreover, to keep up his strength, he was provided with six extra tongues apart from the one in his mouth, to lick up the butter offered to him in sacrifices.

Agni didn't demand too much from his devotees and so was a popular god. Lovers and men seeking to enhance their masculinity worshipped Agni and he never failed to grant them their desires.

Naturally, more and more people offered prayers and sacrifices to Agni and soon he had consumed so many oblations that he became fat and lazy and lost his strength to blaze and burn. All it needed was a light drizzle to put his flames out. And each time he was invoked by his devotees, he found it more and more difficult to make an appearance.

What Agni didn't realize until much later was that the king of gods, Indra, had become jealous of Agni's popularity and had been looking for a way to humiliate him. Knowing that Agni had lost his strength to stand up to rain and wind and still burn tall and proud, Indra always sent a few rain clouds to put out the sacrificial fire.

'What shall I do now, Father?' Agni asked Brahma. 'I am unable to stand up to Indra. He turns up at each one of my sacrifices and ruins it. Unless I am allowed to complete a sacrifice

I will not be able to regain my strength, and each time the sacrificial fire goes out, my devotees begin to lose faith in me.'

Brahma sighed, 'When I gave you seven tongues, it was to help you build up your strength. Instead you became greedy and ate up everything that was offered to you. You are paying for your greed.'

Agni fell at Brahma's feet and pleaded, 'I promise never to lose control again but please help me regain my energy.'

Brahma looked at Agni and decided that he was truly remorseful and meant every word. So he said, 'Go to Khandavaprastha. Krishna and Arjuna need your assistance. They will protect you from Indra. But even as you help them, remember that you could cause the other creatures there much harm. Do what you have to, but carefully, and when you finish, you will regain your powers!'

Once upon a time, Khandavaprastha had been a glorious city ruled by kings like Puruvas, Nahusa and Yayati. But the city had become a ruin now and in its place was a forest full of thorns and bushes. Birds and animals, thieves and bandits and murderers had all made it their home. So dense was the forest that those who dared to go in never found their way back.

Hoping to settle once and for all the quarrel between the Pandavas and Kauravas, Dhritarashtra divided Hastinapura. He gave the Pandavas the ruins and the forest of Khandavaprastha. It was here that the Pandavas had to build their empire.

Arjuna stood at the edge of the forest looking very worried. 'How do we build a kingdom here?' he asked Krishna.

Krishna smiled mischievously and said, 'Make an offering to Agni and he will be here to help you tame this wilderness.'

Arjuna set about preparing for a sacrifice to worship Agni. Krishna watched him and said, 'No butter or ghee is to be offered to Agni. He has eaten so much in the past few days that he has indigestion and will not appear anywhere food is offered. You need to light the fire with wood and scented herbs and it will burn by itself.'

So Arjuna did as Krishna told him to and Agni appeared. He rubbed his stomach that stuck out like a little round hill and said, 'Arjuna, I will help you tame this forest but you have to protect me from Indra's rain clouds as I go about my task. I do not have the power to blaze and burn as I used to. Even a little rain cloud can put me out!'

Arjuna, who was Indra's son, beseeched his father not to interrupt the mission and let Agni burn the forest down. Indra hid his irritation and agreed to stay away. So Agni unleashed his flames. At first, the fire burnt slowly and quietly but as his strength grew, the fire began to blaze furiously. Agni laughed in glee and leapt from branch to branch, from tree to tree, consuming the wood of the forest.

All the birds and animals fled the forest and the wicked men died in its flames. Just then, Agni heard a faint cry, 'O fire god, O Agni, we are helpless. Please do not harm us!'

He looked around wondering if it was one of Indra's ways to trick him. Then he spotted a tree with a nest and in it were four baby birds. They were much too young to fly away to safety and had persuaded their mother to leave. Agni heard their cries and remembered what Brahma had said. So he left that tree untouched and burnt everything else.

When the mother bird returned, she saw her children were safe and she blessed Agni that he would never lose his strength again. Thus Agni regained his power and the Pandavas built their kingdom of Indraprastha on the ruins of Khandavaprastha.

What Draupadi Did to Feed
Ten Thousand Sages

After another game of dice with the Kauravas, Yudhishtira lost his kingdom. He was forced to go into exile with his four brothers and Draupadi. During this time, he performed many penances. The sun god was so pleased by Yudhishtira's austerities that he appeared before him bearing in his hands a wonderful gift. 'Yudhishtira,' he said, 'this is the akshayapatra, the vessel of plenty. This will provide you all the food you and your family need for the next twelve years. It will fill up as soon as the food in it is consumed. However, once Draupadi eats her share of the food, the vessel will stay empty till the next day.'

During their time in exile in the forests, the Pandavas were visited by many people. Kings and sages, scholars and warriors all flocked to the Pandavas' simple home in the forests. No matter how many people came to see them, all the guests were looked after with great care and fed as much food as they wanted. This was possible because of the akshayapatra.

The Kauravas, especially Duryodhana, were very peeved to hear about how the Pandavas managed to extend such hospitality in spite of having very little to call their own.

One day, the sage Durvasa came to visit Duryodhana, accompanied by his ten thousand disciples. Since the sage's short temper was well known, Duryodhana lavished much attention on the sage and his disciples.

Durvasa was immensely pleased and said, 'You have been very devoted. I haven't had such a wonderful welcome anywhere else. Ask me for any boon.'

Duryodhana sighed in relief. Then he suddenly had an idea. He would use this opportunity to add to the Pandavas' misery.

He cast down his eyes and spoke humbly, 'Your Holiness is very kind to offer me a boon when I was only doing my duty. My only wish is that you visit my cousins in the forest and honour them with your presence. Perhaps it would be best if you went late in the evening.'

Duryodhana knew from his spies that every day the Pandavas fed their guests first, then the brothers ate their share and only then did Draupadi eat. But all this was completed early in the evening, as the Pandavas rose and slept with the sun.

When Durvasa and his ten thousand disciples reached the Pandavas' home, it was late evening. Draupadi had already eaten, washed the akshayapatra and put it away.

The Pandavas received the sage warmly, not knowing that Draupadi had already eaten. The sage smiled at them and said, 'My disciples and I will bathe in the river. We are very hungry. Please ensure that the food is ready by the time we come back.'

When the Pandavas came to tell Draupadi of their new guests, she wrung her hands in despair. She did not know what to do. Durvasa's temper was renowned, and he could quite easily curse them for not giving him food.

Finally, not knowing what to do, she folded her hands and prayed, 'Krishna, only you can help me now.'

Krishna appeared before her. He said, 'I don't know why but I feel a great hunger. Bring me something to eat and then we shall solve your problem.'

Draupadi stared at Krishna in shock. What was wrong with him? Here she was asking him for help on how to feed the sage and his disciples, and he wanted food instead! Didn't he understand that there was nothing to eat? 'There is nothing to eat. The akshayapatra is empty. Which is why I asked you for help,' she cried.

'Go, Draupadi,' Krishna said with a smile. 'Go bring me that vessel.'

Draupadi gave him the akshayapatra. Krishna peered inside. 'Aha!' he said triumphantly. 'What do we have here? You said you cleaned the vessel but what is this?' He held up a grain of rice and a shred of vegetable.

Draupadi looked at her feet ashamed. He must think she was a slovenly creature incapable of even cleaning a vessel.

Krishna merely smiled again and put the grain of rice and vegetable into his mouth. When Draupadi looked up, he seemed satisfied with that.

'Bhimasena,' he called, 'go tell the sage and his disciples that the food is ready.' Bhima stared in surprise at the empty vessel. He wondered what Krishna meant but went anyway.

Meanwhile, as the sage and his disciples finished bathing, they suddenly felt their hunger disappear. Not only were they not hungry, they felt really full and replete, as if they had just finished a large banquet.

'Master, we cannot eat anything more,' the disciples told Durvasa.

Durvasa, too, felt as if he couldn't eat even one mouthful.

Just then Bhima arrived to summon them to dinner.

Durvasa rubbed his stomach and told Bhima, 'It is strange but we are not hungry any more. Our apologies, but we will come another day.' And so they left.

Bhima smiled. By eating that one grain of rice, Krishna had satisfied their hunger, he realized. And so Duryodhana's plan to invoke the sage's wrath came to nothing.

How Agastya Killed the Rakshasas

From his ashram on Mount Kunjara, the sage Agastya kept the demons under control. He let them roam freely wherever they wanted but as soon as they tried to conquer a region or its people, he would step in and destroy them.

The rakshasas Vatapi and Ilwala were brothers. They lived in the Dandaka forest. The wily brothers, who possessed many special powers, frequently tried many tricks on sages and other human beings, but Agastya always saw through them and punished them.

One night Ilwala and Vatapi were sitting under a tree. 'This is so terrible,' Ilwala grumbled. 'We are supposed to be rakshasas but we might as well be sheep. That Agastya has such a tight control over us that we can't do a thing.'

'What do you want to do?' Vatapi asked, amused by his brother's expression.

Ilwala smacked his lips, rubbed his hands and said, 'I'd like to kill a few hermits and I'd like to see every sage in the forest quake in fear when they hear our names.'

Vatapi thought for a while and said, 'I have an idea.'

The next day Ilwala disguised himself as a rich merchant and, leading a handsome ram, went to a hermitage. 'Noble sages,' he said, bending low and speaking in a very respectful tone, 'I would like to gift this ram to you. He is the finest ram in my herd and it would please me greatly if you were to accept him.

He is worthy of a sacrifice…look at him. See how his horns curl so elegantly. Look at his eyes, they seem ready to face anything. There is neither fear nor stupidity there.'

The hermits examined the ram and decided to use the animal for their sacrifice. 'We are very thankful to you,' they said. 'You will be blessed for this generous gesture. What can we do for you?'

Ilwala looked at his feet and said, 'I do not need anything. Except that you let me stay here till the end of the sacrifice.'

The hermits agreed and went to prepare for the sacrifice. Soon the ram was led to the altar. After the sacrifice, it was usual to cook the ram and eat it as part of the ceremonial food.

Ilwala stood quietly, watching the hermits eat. When the last morsel was consumed, he clapped his hands. 'Brother Vatapi,' he called, 'please make your appearance.'

Vatapi, for it was he who had taken the form of the ram, tore through the stomachs of the hermits and came forth. As he emerged, all his different body parts magically joined together again so that he was whole.

Ilwala and Vatapi looked at the dead hermits and rolled on the ground in glee.

'Vatapi, you are so clever!' Ilwala giggled.

'Oh, what did I do?' Vatapi said blinking his eyelids coyly. 'How can you blame me if the hermits had a spot of indigestion.'

Ilwala giggled some more, 'But I never knew indigestion could kill.'

Vatapi sighed and said, 'Now you know. What is it they say—you learn something new every day.'

Again and again, the two brothers tricked the hermits and killed them.

One day Vatapi said, 'This is getting to be boring. These

hermits, despite being so learned, are quite foolish and are tricked easily. I think it's time we found someone who's a little smarter than these fools. Let's try the trick on Agastya and rid the world of him.' Ilwala scratched his head and said, 'Are you sure? He is not like the others…'

'If you are such a coward then we won't,' Vatapi said.

'It's not that…' Ilwala began.

'Then don't make a fuss.'

So the next day Ilwala dressed as a nobleman and went to Agastya's hermitage leading a ram. As usual, he made a present of the ram to Agastya, who received it with a smile.

When the sacrifice was performed and Agastya had eaten the meat of the ram, Ilwala clapped his hands and said, 'Brother Vatapi, please come out.'

But there was no sign of Vatapi.

Ilwala clapped again and called in a louder voice. There was still no response.

Ilwala began to get nervous. He yelled out his brother's name. But Vatapi still didn't appear.

By now Ilwala was really scared and he called again in a trembling voice, 'Brother Vatapi come out.'

Agastya patted his round stomach and said, 'I don't think you realize how strong my gastric juices are. Even as I eat, my food is digested. Perhaps that is why I never have indigestion. Though I must confess that the taste of the meat I just ate makes me want to never eat ram again.'

Ilwala looked at him horrified. Agastya continued to rub his stomach and said, 'You think you are so clever but I knew what you were up to the moment you appeared at my doorstep. Your brother will never play his trick again. Do you hear me? Your brother has been digested!'

Ilwala lost his temper at that and raised his leg to kick the sage and trample him. But Agastya raised his eyes and opened them wide and stared at Ilwala. The fire from his eyes burnt Ilwala to a little heap of ash.

Thus the Dandaka forest was rid of the rakshasa brothers.

Kacha and Devayani

Long ago, the Devas and the Asuras fought all the time for the lordship of the three worlds. The Asuras were carefree and happy as long as Shukracharya, their preceptor, was with them. The valiant Devas, tired of the unequal struggle, went to Kach, the handsome son of Brihaspati, preceptor of the Devas and asked him to go to Shukracharya and learn the secret of Mritasanjibani.

The obedient and dutiful Kacha immediately set out to meet Shukracharya. He humbly presented himself before the great wise man, introduced himself as the son of Brihaspati, and asked to become his disciple.

Shukracharya was a true teacher. He immediately recognised Kacha's brilliance as a student. Shukracharya did not differentiate between his students. He gave Kacha a warm welcome and accepted him as his pupil.

Shukracharya had a daugher, Devayani, whom he loved dearly. He introduced Kacha to his daughter saying, 'Kacha has vowed to be my pupil till the period of his studies is over.'

All learning in those days was handed down by word of mouth. The pupil lived with his guru's family as one of the household. In return for his education, the pupil served his guru with love and devotion. However, Shukracharya was very busy either at court or he was deep in meditation. So Kacha helped Devayani with her daily chores and watched after her.

Within a few days of his arrival, Kacha found himself

spending all his leisure hours in the company of the lively Devayani. Devayani was slowly drawn towards Kacha and they fell in love.

Shukracharya liked Kacha because he was an attentive disciple.

As the years passed, the Asuras became suspicious of Kacha. They wanted to get rid of him. One day as Kacha was attending Shukracharya's cattle, the Asuras fell upon him and slew him. Then they cut him into pieces and fed his flesh to their dogs.

When Kacha did not come home at the normal hour, Devayani became alarmed. When the cattle came back without Kacha she ran in a panic to her father and told him that Kacha was missing. Shukracharya closed his eyes and to the great relief of Devayani, Kacha came back to life and appeared before her. When Devayani inquired about his disappearance, Kacha tried to explain in a puzzled voice, 'I was killed by the Asuras but I do not know how I came back to life?' Shukracharya just smiled.

The love between Kacha and Devayani grew day by day. The Asuras were worried. They guessed right, Kacha was there to learn the secret of Mritasanjibani.

One day Devayani asked Kacha to get her a particular flower that only grows in the deep forest. Kacha went for it. The Asuras followed him and once again killed him. But this time they carried his body to a secluded spot, grounded up into a paste, and dissolved it in the water of the ocean.

Devayani waited and waited. When Kacha did not return she went again to her father. Shukracharya meditated and once again used the secret knowledge to revive Kacha. Devayani was overjoyed.

The Asuras were now at their wits end. 'How can we kill Kacha? Every time we kill him, his guru brings him to life!'

They went to one of the senior Asuras and asked him how to destroy Kacha for good. The senior Asura gave them an idea. The next day, when Kacha went out with the cattle, they again slew him. This time then burnt him in the jungle. Then they took the ashes home and mixed it in a wine which Shukracharya was very fond of. They took the drink to Shukracharya for a taste. Shukracharya loved it. He immediately drank it and blessed the Asuras.

When the cattle once again returned home without Kacha Devayani knew what had happened.

'Will Kacha ever be mine?' she asked herself, 'The Asuras will never leave him alone!'

She went to Shukracharya and wept. 'Father, without Kacha I am as good as dead, please bring him back to life.'

Shukracharya waited for a while thinking. 'It is no good to bring Kacha to life. The Asuras will only kill him again.'

He tried to console his daughter, 'It is futile Devayani to bring Kacha to life. The Asuras are determined to get rid of him. A wise soul, like you, should not grieve at a loved one's death. You are young and beautiful and you have your own life to live.'

But Devayani was adamant. Very strong was her love for Kacha.

'Father' she said, 'Kacha was your best student. I am in love with him. I can not live without him.'

Devayani stopped eating. Shukracharya could no longer bear to see his daughter in such agony. Again Shukracharya used his secret knowledge and called upon Kacha to come back to the world of the living. Kacha came back to life and spoke from inside the stomach of Shukracharya.

'The Asuras killed me but I do not know how I happen to be inside your stomach?' echoed Kacha.

Shukracharya cursed himself for drinking the wine given by the Asuras. 'Henceforth, wine shall be forbidden for those engaged in the pursuit of wisdom,' declared Shukracharya in great frustration. Now Shukracharya had a real dilemma of his own. He could ask Kacha to come out but that would mean his own death.

When he told Devayani of his dilemma she was again adamant, 'Father, I cannot live if either of you dies.'

After long deliberation Shukracharya thought of a way out. He knew now the real purpose of Kacha's visit. He addressed Kacha, 'I now see why you came and truly you have succeeded. There is only one way by which both of us can ensure Devayani's happiness. I will have to teach you the craft of Mritasanjivani.'

With his new knowledge, Kacha emerged from Shukracharya's dying body and then immediately brought his guru back to life. Shukracharya could not have been happier with his pupil's progress.

When the Asuras came to offer him wine, Shukracharya shouted, 'You fools! Kacha now knows my secret. You helped him learn by your foolish deeds. But rest assured Kacha will continue to live with me because of his love for Devayani.'

But Shukracharya was wrong. Kacha too faced the troubling dilemma. Waiting for the period of his studies to come to an end, Kacha kept silent. While his love for Devayani was deep, his sense of duty towards the devas was no less strong.

On the last the day of his studies, Kacha went to Shukracharya for his blessing. As a wise man and a dedicated teacher, Shukracharya concealed his grudge against Kacha but he was wondering how Kacha was going to bid farewell to Devayani.

Devayani waited for Kacha to propose marriage. But when Kacha broke the heartbreaking news that he was going to fulfil his obligations to his own people, her joy turned to tears. Devayani pleaded with Kacha to take her as his wife. But Kacha replied, 'Peerless one! I was reborn in your father's stomach. I am therefore your brother. I can't marry you. I must return to heaven.'

The broken-hearted Devayani cried out in her grief. She accused Kacha of using her to attain his goal. Distort she cursed Kacha, 'You will never be able to use the craft of Mritasanjivani.'

Kacha quietly listened and then spoke, 'Devayani, it is wrong to curse me. I could have walked away without reviving your father. There is no doubt that my love was sincere and truthful. But, I also have a duty to perform towards my own people. Because of your unfairness to me, I am cursing you. No Rishi's son will ever marry you. I may still teach the craft of Mritasanjivani to others, even though I may not be able to use it myself.' Saying this Kacha departed for the abode of Indra, king of the Devas. Shukhacharya gently led Devayani away.

With the passage of time, Devayani completely forgot about Kacha. She once again became playful and lived happily with her father and her playmates in the city of Vrishaparva, king of the Asuras. Of her playmates, the most important was princess Sharmistha, the daughter of King Vrishaparva.

The Enlightened Butcher

Kaushika was his parents' only son.

'Mother,' he said one day, 'I want to go off into the jungle and devote myself to spiritual studies.'

His mother said with concern, 'But son, your father and I are very old. Your father is so sick he can hardly move. If you go away, what will happen to us? Who will attend to our needs?'

Kaushika did not listen. He was determined to study the Vedas. His mother cried in vain as she watched her son turn his back on her and leave for the jungle.

Eventually Kaushika acquired great mystical powers.

One afternoon, as he was meditating under a tree, a crane flew up, and perched herself on a branch above Kaushika. Some bird droppings fell on Kaushika's head. Kaushika furiously threw a fiery gaze at the crane.

The crane immediately fell dead.

The sage felt sorry for what he had done. 'How could I have allowed my anger to take over me that way?' he mourned.

Later in the day, he went to a village to beg for alms. The lady of the house asked him to wait and went to get some food. Right then her husband arrived. She immediately set aside the pot of food she was taking to the sage and went to attend her husband.

After washing his feet, giving him food, and attending to his needs, she came back out to give the alms to the sage. The sage was very insulted. 'You put your husband before a pious sage? Do you know the power of a Brahmin?'

She calmly replied, 'Yes, a true Brahmin is he who has mastered his anger. Please do not threaten me. I am not a crane that will die by your fiery gaze.'

The sage was amazed. 'How does she know about the crane?' he wondered.

The lady continued, 'Oh holy one! You are a learned Brahmin but you have not understood the truth about virtue. If you want to be enlightened, go to Dharmavyadha who lives in Mathura. Anyone will tell you where he lives.'

The sage thanked the lady and hurried to Mathura. 'He must be a great and learned sage indeed,' Kaushika thought to himself.

But when he finally reached Dharmavyadaha's place, he found it to be a butcher shop!

A very ordinary looking man came out and said, 'Welcome holy one. I am Dharmavyadaha, the man you seek.'

'How can a butcher be spiritually enlightened?' Kaushika asked in amazement.

Dharmavyadaha smiled and said with compassion, 'I know the story of the crane and of the woman who sent you here. Come, let us go to my house.'

The sage could not contain himself and blurted out, 'But butchering animals is such a sinful profession! Are you not ashamed?'

'I am not,' the butcher calmly said. 'I am engaged in a family trade. I work hard and honestly at it. There is no reason for me to be ashamed of my work!'

'Holy one,' continued the butcher. 'If I do injury to other creatures, so do you as you did to the crane.'

'As we walk on the soil, we are trampling on numerous

creatures. Nor is the air devoid of creatures.'

'You see that farmer tilling the land? He is killing so many animals that thrive under the soil.'

They reached the butcher's house. The butcher's wife was doing her household chores and his two boys were playing.

The butcher introduced the sage to his wife and boys.

Then the butcher entered the house and touched his parents' feet.

'Here is a learned Brahmin who has come from a far-off place,' the butcher told his old father.

'Welcome, holy one,' the father said.

Before leaving the room, the butcher remarked, 'My parents are my Gods. My wife and my children attend to them with devotion and love. We consider caring for them to be our greatest duty.'

'In doing one's duty cheerfully lies true virtue. This is what the dutiful wife sent you to learn.'

'Oh learned one!' the butcher continued, 'You have run away from your responsibilities and deserted your aged father and mother. Spiritual achievement is useless if one has neglected one's Dharma, or duties.'

The sage remembered his mother crying, 'Who will look after us when you are gone my son?'

The sage apologised, 'You have shown me the path of true virtue, the true meaning of Dharma, Oh pious one. I am deeply indebted to you.'

Kaushika immediately returned to his parents and served them lovingly till the end of their days.

The Beginning of the Mahabharata

The story of Mahabharata starts with King Dushyant, a powerful ruler of ancient India. Dushyanta married Shakuntala, the foster-daughter of sage Kanva. Shakuntala was born to Menaka, a nymph of Indra's court, from sage Vishwamitra, who secretly fell in love with her. Shakuntala gave birth to a worthy son Bharata, who grew up to be fearless and strong. He ruled for many years and was the founder of the Kuru dynasty. Unfortunately, things did not go well after the death of Bharata and his large empire was reduced to a kingdom of medium size with its capital Hastinapur.

Mahabharata means the story of the descendents of Bharata. The regular saga of the epic of the Mahabharata, however, starts with king Shantanu. Shantanu lived in Hastinapur and was known for his valour and wisdom.

One day he went out hunting to a nearby forest. Reaching the bank of the river Ganges (Ganga), he was startled to see an indescribably charming damsel appearing out of the water and then walking on its surface. Her grace and divine beauty struck Shantanu at the very first sight and he was completely spellbound.

When the king inquired who she was, the maiden curtly asked, 'Why are you asking me that?'

King Shantanu admitted 'Having been captivated by your loveliness, I, Shantanu, king of Hastinapur, have decided to marry you.'

'I can accept your proposal provided that you are ready to

abide by my two conditions,' argued the maiden.

'What are they?' anxiously asked the king.

'First, you will never ask anything about my personal life, like who I am or where do I come from? Secondly, you will never stop me from doing anything or ask the reason of anything I do.'

Shantanu was totally gripped by the maiden's beauty, now known as Ganga, and immediately accepted her conditions. They instantly entered into a love marriage (Gandharvavivah) and returned home.

Things went on quite smoothly for sometime and then queen Ganga gave birth to a lovely boy. As soon as king Shantanu heard of this good news, he was overjoyed and rushed to the palace to congratulate the queen. But he was astonished to see that the queen took the newborn into her arms, went to the river, and drowned him. The king was shocked and felt miserable, yet he could not ask the queen about her action. He was bound by his pledge, not to question or interfere with the her actions.

Hardly had Shantanu recovered from the shock of the death of his first son at the hands of the queen when she became expectant again. The king felt happy and thought that the queen would not repeat her dreadful action again. But the queen again took the newborn into her arms, and drowned him in the river.

After seeing the ghastly action of the queen, the king was in immense grief again, but his pledge barred him to say anything.

This continued on until queen Ganga bore the eighth son and marched to the river as before. Shantanu lost his patience and as soon as the queen was about to drown the newborn, Shantanu stopped her. 'I have lost seven sons like this and am left with no heir. I can no longer stand to see my flesh and blood decimated before my eyes.'

Queen Ganga turned around and said, 'Oh king, you have violated your pledge. I will not stay with you any longer. However before leaving you, I will open the secret that led to the death of your seven sons. Once it so happened that the saint Vashishtha got offended with eight gods known as Vasus. He cursed them to be born as human beings on the earth and undergo the mental torture of being a human. Hearing this, seven of the Vasus implored the saint to be excused but the eighth one, who was the most mischievous, kept standing rudely.'

Vashishtha was appeased and modified his curse, 'Seven of you will die and come back to heaven as soon as you are born, but the eighth one will have to live on the earth for a long period and face the tribulations as a human.'

Ganga continued, 'Upon the request from the Vasus, I assumed the human form and married you. My job is now over and I must now go back to my heavenly abode. I am taking your eighth son with me and will bring him back to you after he is amply grown up.'

After saying this, Ganga flew away into the sky along with the newborn. King Shantanu felt very disappointed and returned to his palace with a broken heart.

Many years after, when Shantanu was taking a stroll on the bank of the river Ganges (Ganga), Goddess Ganga emerged out of the river with a young boy.

Ganga spoke, 'Oh king! Here is your eighth son, Deva Vrata. I have brought him up in order that he may be able to cope with what is to befall on him in his life on this earth.'

The king happily brought the prince to the palace and celebrated his advent by declaring him the crown prince of his kingdom. Deva Vrata was brave, just and looked highly promising.

King Shantanu was getting old and announced his retirement. He was lonely and always missed Ganga. It was one day while he was taking a stroll on the bank of the river Ganges, he was attracted towards a charming maiden, Satyavati. She was the daughter of the chief of the fishermen tribe. She took the sages across the river on her boat. She had a divine aroma coming out of her body.

Shantanu did not know the secret that circled around Satyavati during her maiden days. Satyavati once had a bad fishy smell on her body. Sage Parashar, one of the sages who she took across the river, had a special liking for her. He was pleased and blessed her with a sweet aroma along with the boon of a son who was named Vyas. Immediately after birth, Vyas grew up quickly through his divine powers and left for the forest. Vyas, however, promised his mother Satyavati that he will come back whenever he was called for. Vyas, later known as Veda Vyas, had mastery of the Vedas but was extremely ugly looking and had a horrible smell. Veda Vyas authored the story of the Mahabharata, for the sake of the posterity. It is said that Vyas dictated the entire epic at a stretch while Lord Ganesh acted as the scriber. In addition, Vyas played a central role in his story appearing and disappearing on the scene whenever his mother or her family members sought his help. He had rare magical qualities to resolve their problems.

Shantanu, unaware of the secrets of Satyavati's maiden life, was charmed by her beauty. He went to her father, the chief fisherman, and asked him for the hand of his daughter. The chief fisherman, placed the condition that the son born of Satyavati will be the successor of the Kaurava throne and not Deva Vrata. Santanu was shocked to hear the condition and returned home disappointed and unhappy. Deva Vrata later discovered the cause of his father's unhappiness and went to Satyavati's father, to advocate his father's position on marrying Satyavati. In return he promised to give up his right to the throne for Satyavati's son.

The chief fisherman thought for a while and showed his further concern by saying, 'What about your children? They may not honour your promise.'

Hearing this, Deva Vrata took the terrible vow that he will never marry in his life, he would remain a brahamachari. From then on he was known as Bheeshma, the firm. Bheeshma brought Satyavati on his chariot to the palace and presented her to his father. Shantanu felt shocked when he heard of all that happened. He blessed Bheeshma with the power to choose his day of death.

In due course of time, queen Satyavati became the mother of two princes—Chitrangad and Vichitravirya. After Shantanu's death, Chitrangad succeeded the throne but was killed in a war. Vichitravirya, was then a minor, and was enthroned by Bheeshma as the king of Hastinapur. When Vichitravirya came of age, Bheeshma and queen Satyavati got him married to two princesses of Kashi, Amba and Ambika. Unfortunately, Vichitravirya died without a successor.

Bheeshma and Satyavati conferred and decided to call Veda Vyas. Vyas arrived in no time. Satyavati explained to him the grave situation that the Kaurava family was facing without an heir. She requested Vyas to bless Ambika, the elder of the two widows of Vichitravirya, with a son who can succeed the deceased king. Vyas agreed.

When Vyas approached Ambika, she was frightened by his ugly face and shut her eyes while the saint uttered the boon. As a result, the son born to Ambika was blind. He was named Dhritarashtra. The queen was disappointed and asked Vyas to offer the boon to Ambalika, the younger widow. Ambalika could not stand his smell and turned pale out of fear while the saint was uttering the boon. As a result, the child born of Ambalika was pale and was called Pandu, meaning pale.

Queen Satyavati was puzzled; what can be done now? Requesting the saint for another chance, she sent for the elder widow Ambika once more to receive the boon from the saint. Ambika was so scared of the saint that she could not dare to go before him. Instead, without telling her mother-in-law, Ambika sent her maid to the saint after disguising her with stately garments. The maid remained fearless and greeted the saint, Veda Vyas, with great devotion. Feeling happy, the saint gave her a boon and she bore a perfect child called Vidur.

In course of time, Pandu ascended the throne as his elder brother Dhritarashtra was blind and Vidur became the prime minister due to his sagacity and distinguished talent. Dhritarashtra married Gandhari, the princess of Gandhar in Beluchistan (today's Pakistan). When Gandhari came to know that her husband is blind, she, as a true wife, sharing the emotions of her husband, bandaged her eyes permanently with a cloth.

During the time of Pandu, the kingdom of the Kurus expanded far and wide. Pandu was married twice, first to Kunti and then to Madri. After many years of rule, Pandu decided to retire to Himalayas leaving the kingdom in the hands of Dhritarashtra and grandfather Bheeshma. There was no heir to the throne since none of the brothers had any children.

Later one day, when Pandu was hunting in the forest, he shot an arrow at a deer who was in the state of making love. Before dying, the deer cursed Pandu that he will die instantly when he will touch any of his wives. Pandu was shocked. After returning to the hermitage, he explained what happened to his wives. They all agreed to lead the life of an ascetic. They were, however, sad that any chance of having their children to succeed the throne of Kaurava dynasty was gone.

In Hastinapur, Gandhari called Veda Vyasa and requested him the boon to bear one hundred sons and a daughter. Veda Vyas very kindly agreed but informed Gandhari that it will take some time before they arrive. Gandhari was in no rush since she knew that Pandu could not have any children because of the deer's curse. However, things turned out differently.

In the forest, Pandu began to suffer from a deep depression, due to the deer's curse. Kunti painfully noticed it. Kunti was concerned and wanted to reveal a secret that she kept in her heart until then, in order to make Pandu happy.

Kunti said, 'When I was a young maid, sage Durbasha came to my father's house. I served the sage devotionally and, as a result, the sage blessed me with a mantra through which I could invoke any god I desire to get a son. The mantra, however, can be used only five times.'

Pandu was very happy. He can now have his sons without even touching Kunti. Kunti, however, did not disclose to Pandu that she has already used the mantra once. This happened when, after receiving the mantra, she became impatient to use it without comprehending the consequences. She called the sun god and was blessed with a son wearing earrings from birth. Now she realized that the child is born out of wedlock. For fear of infamy, she put the newborn into a basket and set it afloat the river Ganga. A charioteer who was childless, luckily discovered the basket. He brought up the abandoned child who was later named Karna because he was born with the earrings.

Pandu requested Kunti to call for Dharma, the god of righteousness. Kunti was blessed with Pandu's first son Yudhishthira. The news of the birth of Pandu's first child reached Dhritarashtra and Gandhari. Gandhari was disturbed that she cannot be the mother of the future king. She immediately called Vyasa and requested him to force the birth of her hundred sons. Through his magical powers, Vyasa shortened the waiting period and hundred sons of Dhritarashtra emerged along with a daughter Dushala. Duryodhan was the eldest son while Dushashan was the second. Gandhari was not happy that, in spite of her best efforts, Pandu's first son Yudhishthira would be the true heir to the throne and not her eldest son, Duryodhana.

In order to strengthen the Kuru dynasty, Pandu requested Kunti for more children. Kunti called the wind god Pavan and Bheema, the second son, was born. Indra blessed Kunti with the third son, Arjuna. Madri was still childless. Pandu requested Kunti to pass on the mantra to Madri so that she can have a child. Madri called the twin god, Ashwins and was blessed with two sons, Nakula and Sahadeva.

Thus Pandu had five sons, Yudhishthira, Bheema, Arjuna, Nakula and Sahadeva. These five worthy children of Pandu were called Pandavas. They grew up strong and well behaved. They learnt the art of war games from their able father Pandu. The sages taught them the teachings of the Vedas.

It was one spring day while Pandu was strolling on the riverside, he saw Madri passing by. Aroused with passion he touched Madri and died instantly. Kunti and Madri were devastated. The news reached Dhritarashtra and he, too, was shocked. The body of Pandu was carried to Hastinapur for the crematory rites. Madri decided to ascend to the funeral pyre of Pandu and appealed to Kunti to take care of her two sons, Nakula and Sahadeva, like her own three children. The Pandavas, the sons of Pandu, returned to Hastinapur and joined their cousins, Kauravas, the sons of Dhritarashtra.

All the cousins, the Pandavas and the Kauravas, grew up

together under the direction of their grandfather Bheeshma. Kripacharya, an able teacher of martial art, trained them for war games.

Kripacharya in his childhood days, known as Kripa, came to King Shantanu, Bheeshma's father, along with his sister Kripi, as orphans from a Brahmin family. Shantanu was a kind-hearted person. He raised Kripa and Kripi with best care. Kripa, through his best effort became a master in martial art and was then known as Kripacharya. Kripi was married to Drona, the son of sage Bharadwaj; Sage Bharadwaj was the best archer of his time. He ran a school to teach martial arts to the princes. His father, Bharadwaj, personally trained his son Drona. During his student life, Drona became a close friend of prince Drupada who promised Drona that he would share his kingdom with him when he became king. But when Drupada became king, he forgot all about his childhood promises to Drona.

After the death of Bharadwaj, Drona took over his father's responsibilities and was known as Dronacharya. In those days, an ideal teacher provided free education to all of his students and was satisfied with the honour showered by his students and the community. As a result, he stayed poor in meeting his daily needs unless some royalty provided financial support. Drona was no exception. He had a son named Ashwathama whom he loved dearly. One day Dronacharya witnessed that his playmates mocked his son because he was poor. He decided to go to his former schoolmate Drupada for financial help. Drupada, drowned in his royalty, ignored his childhood promises to Drona. He insulted Drona in his open court. Drona took the vow that one day he will get even with Drupada and left the court in rage. He soon left his hermitage and arrived at Kripa's residence along with his wife Kripi and Ashwathama.

Drona was passing by one day, when the princes of Hastinapur were playing ball. He saw the bouncing ball fall into a nearby well. The princes were puzzled as to get the ball out of the well. Then Drona came forward. He listened to the princes and then threw his own ring into the well. Then he boasted that he would get both the ball and the ring with the help of his archery. The princes were amazed to see that he kept his promise. They all requested Drona to see their grandfather Bheeshma. Bheeshma, the old warrior, heard what happened and was amazed by the ability of Drona. He immediately appointed Drona as the teacher of archery for the princes. Drona was very pleased with his position that considerably improved the economic condition of his family. He began to instruct the princes with great care and love. He was confident that his royal disciples will one day help him to defeat Drupada, and he will be able to fulfil his vow of getting even with him.

Of all the disciples, Drona loved Arjuna the most. He was most skilful and Drona promised Arjuna that he would make him the best archer in the world. One day, prince Ekalavya, son of King Nishad, came to Drona and requested Drona to take him as his disciple. King Nishad belonged to a low caste and Drona was committed only to the royal princes of Kuru dynasty. Thus, Drona refused to take Ekalavya as his disciple. Ekalavya was disappointed but did not lose hope. He went into a deep forest, made an idol of Drona and considering him as his guru, practiced archery daily. Through his devotion and constant practice, Ekalavya excelled in the game of archery.

One day the Kuru princes went hunting in the jungle where Ekalavya lived. Their hunting dog strayed from the party and saw Ekalavya. It began to bark while Ekalavya was busy with his practice of archery. Ekalavya shot a volley of arrows at the dog such that it corked its open mouth. The dog ran back to the royal party and the princes were amazed to see its plight. They all came to Ekalavya, along with Drona, in order to identify the person who has surpassed them in the art of archery.

Seeing Drona, Ekalavya fell at the feet of his guru. Drona was highly pleased by his devotion and diligence. He soon recognised that Ekalavya will eventually become the indomitable rival of Arjuna and Drona may not be able to keep his promise. So, Drona asked for his right thumb as teacher's reward (guru dakshina) and Ekalavya obeyed, cutting his right thumb and placing it at the guru's feet. What a glorious example of obedience to teachers!

When the princes had completed their training, grandsire Bheeshma arranged for a competition in order to demonstrate their sportsmanship. Various dignitaries were invited in the grand ceremony. Arjuna surprised everyone by his feats of archery. When the tournament was about to complete, Karna arrived on the scene. No one knew that he was the illegitimate child of Kunti raised by a charioteer. He challenged Arjuna. At this point, Kripacharya objected.

'The competition is meant for royal princes only and is not open to ordinary people.'

Hearing the objection, Duryodhan, a rival of Arjuna, came forward and offered Karna the state of Anga, making him a prince. Karna was as good as Arjuna and no one could decide the superiority of one over the other.

The day completed and the royal princes came to Drona to pay respect and pay guru dakshina. Drona asked them to capture Drupada, the king of Panchal, and bring him to Drona as a prisoner. Kauravas and Pandavas had no problem to run over Panchal and present Drupada to Drona.

Drona reminded Drupada of the insults he inflicted on him and said, 'Drupada, as a friend I am returning half of the kingdom to you, but I hope that in the future you will remember the lesson and respect the promises that you make.'

Sati and Siva

In the days of ancient mythology, Brahma, the Prajapati, mentally created ten sons (manasaputra) to carry out his task of creation and destruction. Both Siva and Daksha were the outcome of such a creation but Siva had superior powers. Daksha, however, never liked the supremacy of Siva. So, he took Siva as his rival.

One of the daughters of Daksha, named Sati, was a great devotee of Siva. She was beautiful and virtuous. Most of the time Sati was immersed in the thoughts of Siva and dreamed of being his wife.

Sati, through her sincere and devotional prayers, acquired the blessings of all gods and goddesses. Siva finally yielded and appeared before Sati. She paid her reverence and kneeling down to Siva, chanted in praise of him.

Siva asked her to choose a boon. Siva knew what she would ask but wanted her to speak for herself.

Sati was hesitant, 'How can I say that I want nothing else but Him!'

After a while Sati gathered her courage and started to say, 'Lord will you—'

Siva did not let Sati complete her question, and he blessed her, 'Be my consort, Sati.'

Soon Sati was married to Siva amidst numerous gods and goddesses.

After the wedding, Siva took Sati to Kailash where they spent many a happy days.

Then one day, Siva requested Sati to accompany him to Prayag, today's Allahabad, to attend a fire-worship ceremony or yagna.

When Siva entered the yagna hall, every one stood up to pay respect.

After some time Daksha entered the yagna hall. Everyone stood up to pay respect except Siva. Daksha felt insulted.

'How dare my son-in-law, Siva, not stand up! This is a deliberate insult to me,' Daksha said to himself.

Siva, on the other hand, thought to himself, 'Being a superior power, it will not be nice if I stand up, and harm may befall on Daksha.' Siva did not mean to insult Daksha.

Taking this instance as an exception, Daksha promised to insult Siva in public. He hurriedly returned home and declared that he will hold a grand sacrificial ceremony. He invited all gods and goddesses, but deliberately excluded Siva.

When Sati, Siva's beautiful wife and Daksha's daughter, noticed a large procession of gods and goddesses passing by, she curiously asked Siva, 'Where are they going?'

Siva replied, 'To the grand sacrificial ceremony to be held by Daksha, your father.'

Sati was amazed.

'Then why have you not been invited?' she demanded angrily. 'You should have been the first to be asked.'

Siva smiled gently at his wife's loyalty and fervour.

'Daksha has always been hostile to me,' Siva tried to explain.

But Sati's disbelief increased, 'Does my father not realize that you are the supreme power and no one can equal you?'

'You are a good and true wife Sati,' Siva replied gently, 'but Daksha thinks differently, he takes me as his rival.'

'Invited or not,' Sati said furiously, 'I think we should go. It is, after all, my own father's house and I at least need no invitation.'

'Then go with my blessings, Sati,' replied Siva. 'but do not forget that Daksha will shower insults upon me. You must be strong enough to bear it silently and not allow your rage to show in your father's presence. If you are unable to tolerate his insults, I fear you may come to harm.'

Taking Nandi, the gentle white bull who was Siva's companion and mount, Sati arrived at her father's grand sacrificial ceremony.

Daksha reluctantly received her and publicly condemned Siva—calling him the demon of death and an impious haunter of cremation grounds.

'What place has the goblin lord of witches and foul spirits in a sacred ceremony such as mine?' Daksha boomed.

Sati was hurt by his insults to her husband and begged her father to stop, but Daksha could not contain himself.

'It is disgraceful for a so-called god to wear filthy rags, cover himself with snakes and dance like a madman at ceremonies—' continued Daksha on and on, until Sati could not stand any longer. She remembered her husband's caution, 'Do not allow your rage to get over you.'

Sati painfully said, 'I am ashamed to be known as your daughter. As I have promised my husband not to take any revenge, much less upon you, I merely denounce you before this assembly. I shall consume myself in a fire and return to mother Earth until I am born again to a father whom I can respect.'

Daksha ignored the disappearance of Sati and ordered to continue with the sacrifice.

When news reached Siva, through Nandi, that his beloved

wife was dead, he let out a mighty roar that shook Heaven and Earth. He soon created a powerful demon, named Virabhadra, from his matted hair. Siva also created a huge army of demons to accompany Virabhadra. They descended like a hurricane on Daksha's feast, destroying the sacrificial offering and killing all those who dared defend Daksha. Finally every one walked over to Siva's side to seek refuge with him.

Siva was about to destroy the universe, when Brahma came with other gods to calm him down. Siva was still quivering and shook with wrath and grief at the loss of Sati. All the gods soothed the furious Siva and pleaded with him to forgive Daksha and allow him to complete the sacrificial ceremony, which he had started, otherwise he would go to hell.

Relenting, Siva brought back to life all the people who had been killed in the battle and cured all those who had been injured. Finally he looked up, suppressing the power of his destructive third eye, and stated, 'I will return Daksha to life, but he must bear the mark of his foolishness forever.'

The gods agreed to Siva's condition and Daksha was revived. The mark of his foolishness was clear for all to see for instead of his own head, he wore the head of a goat. Daksha fell at Siva's feet weeping with gratitude, and finally acknowledged Siva's supremacy.

With a mighty effort Siva contained his grief for the loss of Sati, and he fell into profound meditation, waiting for the time when she would be reincarnated as Parvati and be his wife once again.

Krishna Janamastami

The festival of Krishna Janamastami is the celebration of Lord Krishna's birthday. Krishna, the eighth incarnation of Lord Vishnu, is a unique character in Hindu mythology. He was naughty in his childhood days, romantic as a young man, and proved to be a profound philosopher in his adulthood as illustrated by the Bhagavad Gita.

The birthday of Krishna falls on the astami of Krishna Paksh (the eighth day of the dark fortnight) in the month of Bhado (July-August), eight days after Raksha Bandhan. The exact date of Krishna's birthday has not been determined but is conjectured to be around 1400 B.C. when the Aryans settled across the Indo-Gangetic plain. It was the rainy season in India and Krishna was born at midnight, in the prison of Kansa, during the middle of a perilous rain and storm. Thus goes the story of Krishna's birth.

Kansa, a despot, was then the king of Mathura. He had imprisoned his father in order to become the king. Devaki was his sister and was married to a noble man, Vasudeva.

Kansa one day heard a heavenly voice, saying, 'Kansa, your days of tyranny will soon be over, you will be killed by the eighth child of Devaki.'

Kansa got frightened. He immediately imprisoned Devaki and Vasudeva. He did not want to take any chance and killed at birth each and every child of Devaki, until the time came for the delivery of the eighth child. To feel more secure, Kansa increased the number of prison guards, kept strict vigilance and put Vasudeva in chains. But God planned otherwise.

At midnight when the eighth child was born, the guards fell fast asleep and Vasudeva's chain fell off his hands and feet. Wasting no time, Vasudeva picked up the newborn baby, and carrying it in a basket, he started towards Gokul. Gokul was a village of cowherds, located across the Yamuna river, where his friend Nanda lived.

It was a dark stormy night with blinding rain continuously pouring from the sky. When Vasudeva reached the river bank of Yamuna, the river was in spate. The wind and storm were blowing wild, and Vasudeva was in a fix.

'Lord, what should I do,' said Vasudeva in a hopeless voice.

Suddenly a miracle happened, the river parted and Vasudeva walked over the river bed. Throughout the way, Vasudeva and the baby were protected from rain by the hood of the great eternal snake, Vasuki. Finally, Vasudeva reached Nanda's house.

Upon reaching Nanda's house, Vasudeva found the mother, Yashoda, and her newborn baby girl in deep sleep. He had no time to think. He quickly exchanged the babies and returned to the prison with the infant girl, while the guards were still asleep.

As soon as Vasudeva entered the prison cell, the door got locked behind him and he was chained again as if nothing happened in between. The guards woke up and heard the cry of the baby. Kansa was immediately informed and he came running to kill the child. But to his utter surprise he found it to be a girl and not a boy, as he expected. Devaki begged for the newborn baby's life from her brother.

'What can a girl do to you Kansa? Spare her life, please!' appealed Devaki, lying at the feet of her brother.

The inhuman Kansa did not pay attention to the appeal. As he was ready to kill the baby by smashing its head on a big boulder, the child slipped out of his hand and flew towards the sky.

At that moment, a heavenly voice was heard, 'Kansa, the one who shall destroy you still lives. He is growing in Gokul.'

Next morning, Nanda and his wife Yashoda discovered the boy, left by Vasudeva, lying in the crib. They were a little puzzled but did not want to fuss about it because they might lose the baby. The baby was of dark complexion, so he was named Krishna.

Kansa was frightened by the heavenly voice. He immediately sent for Putna, his wicked maid, and asked her to kill all the babies born on the same day when Devaki gave birth to the baby. Putna smeared poison on her breast and went around in the town of Gokul to breast-feed the babies born in the month of Bhado. In the beginning people, out of goodness, did not suspect Putna's heinous plans, but as time passed, they found out that all the babies whom Putna fondled were dead. They began to search for Putna. In the meantime, Putna reached Nanda's house and lovingly asked Krishna's mother, Yashoda, to give the baby to her to love and fondle. Yashoda gave the baby and, without any suspicion, went on with her daily chore.

Suddenly there was a loud shriek. Everyone came running to the courtyard and found to their surprise the dead body of Putna lying on the floor while Krishna was smiling and kicking. People now knew that Krishna was not an ordinary boy. Yashoda happily picked up Krishna and felt safe.

Krishna grew in Yashoda's house until he reached his teens. He later challenged Kansa and killed him. Then he released his grandfather Ugrasena and reinstated him to his throne. He respected and loved both his own parents, Vasudeva and Devaki, and his adopted parents, Nanda and Yashoda.

Janamashtami is celebrated with great pomp and show in

Hindu temples and homes in India. The festival is celebrated for two days; on the day when Krishna took birth in the prison of Kansa at Mathura and also on the following day to commemorate Krishna's presence in the house of Nanda and Yashoda at Gokul. Ardent devotees pray in the middle of the night celebrating Krishna's birth on the first day. Children join the celebration on the next day with worships (puja) and sweets (prasad). Decorations depicting Krishna's birth and his transfer to Gokul, are displayed very much the way Christ's birth is displayed during Christmas. This is called jhanki, a peek in the past. In Bengal, it is called, Gupt Vrindavan, meaning hidden Vrindavan, where Krishna spent time with his consort Radha. It is a great fun planning and executing the decoration that depicts Krishna's life in Gokul. The display is left for few days for friends and relatives to enjoy. The grandparents (or other elders) narrate to the children the interesting stories of Krishna, his childhood pranks, romance with Radha in his young days, and finally, his days of kingship offering us the eternal truth of the great Bhagavad Gita. There is nothing in the world that can be compared with the profound philosophy of Gita written in that hoary past.

Ashtavakra

The story of Ashtavakra is taken from the great ancient Indian epic, the Mahabharata. It is the story of a deformed young boy whose intelligence surpassed many old sages of his time.

Sage Uddalaka ran a school (Ashram) teaching Vedic knowledge. Kahoda was one of his best disciples. Uddalaka was so pleased with him that he got his daughter Sujata married to him. Sujata eventually got pregnant and wanted her child to surpass all the sages of his time. So she began to sit in the classes taught by Uddalaka and Kahoda, listening to their chanting with the unborn baby. It was one day, in a class taught by Kahoda, the unborn baby spoke up from inside the womb, 'This is not the way to chant the verse, father.' Kahoda felt insulted in front of the class and cursed, 'You will be born deformed.'

Sujata did not take the instance too seriously and was ambitious. She wanted more money to raise her child the best. So she asked her husband to go to King Janak who was then preparing for a fire worship ceremony (Yagna) hoping that the ceremony will bring money to the family.

When Kahoda approached Janak, the king received him respectfully but said with regret, 'Kahoda, I am unable to perform the Yagna which I decided to perform several years back. Sage Bandhi arrived from nowhere and asked me to start the Yagna only after he is defeated in an academic discussion with the sages participating in the Yagna. His condition further includes that the sages who come forth for the debate, if defeated, will be drowned. So far he has killed many learned sages. Now it is up to you to take the challenge.' Kahoda agreed to debate with Bandhi. He was defeated and drowned in the nearby river. The widowed Sujata heard the news and repented her actions. A few months later, she gave birth to a boy who was deformed at eight joints and so named Ashtavakra. He got his education from his grandfather Uddalaka. Ashtavakra was extremely intelligent and his grandfather loved him dearly and was very proud of him. When Ashtavakra was only twelve, he finished all that he needed to know from his grandfather. He also heard the fate of his father and the Yagna of king Janak, which still remained unfinished as no one could defeat Bandhi.

One night Ashtavakra ran away from the hermitage and came to king Janak. Looking to his deformed body, the guards were amused. Ashtavakra retorted, 'Do not judge a person by his appearance and age, judge him by what he knows. Inform your king that there is a person ready to challenge Bandhi.' The king came and was surprised to see a small deformed boy. He asked a few questions and was greatly impressed by his knowledge. King Janak soon arranged for the debate with Bandhi. When the spectators laughed at seeing the deformed Ashtavakra, Ashtavakra said with anger, 'I did not know that the so-called learned gathering is no better than a bunch of cobblers who judge a person by the skin and not by the knowledge he has.'

To everyone's surprise, Ashtavakara defeated Bandhi in no time. With vengeance he then requested the king to drown his father's killer. Bandhi then disclosed his identity. He said, 'I am the son of Varuna, the god of water. I came to earth on the request of my father to get the best sages from here to perform his twelve years of Yagna. The only way I could get them to my father was to challenge them in a debate and throw them into the water. Now that my father has completed the Yagna; let us go to the river band and watch the sages walk out of the river.'

People rushed to the river bank and watched the sages return from the river. Kahoda came and embraced his learned son Ashtavakra. He then openly admitted that his son Ashtavakra was a lot more intelligent than he. Bandhi then asked Ashtavakra to take a dip in the river, with the blessings of his father, Varuna, which would make him normal. Ashtavakra did as he was told and came out of the river as a handsome young man. Janak rewarded Ashtavakra and Kahoda. They went back to their hermitage to be united with the family. Uddalaka was so happy to see his worthy grandson surpassing in knowledge all the great sages of his time. Sujata rejoiced at seeing her handsome son and her husband.

Breaking the Vanity of Gods

Long long ago, the tyranny of the Ashuras, the evil people, made this earth uninhabitable. The gods, or Devas, were defeated by the Ashuras and they were banished. The gods approached the all-powerful Brahma, the creator of the universe and source of energy for all beings, to help them defeat the Ashuras and bring peace back to the earth. Brahma blessed them and asked them to pursue and fight even harder. The Ashuras were then finally defeated and they fled underground, preying on the opportune moment to rise above again.

The Gods began to celebrate their victory over the Ashuras and became boastful of their power forgetting that it came from the one and only source, Brahma. In fact, they forgot their duties and became engaged in drinking, merrymaking and licentious behaviour. So, to give a lesson, Brahma sent a Yaksha (demigod) to the place where the gods gathered for their celebration party. Indra, the king of the gods and the god of weather, saw the Yaksha approaching them. He asked Agni, the god of fire to inquire who he was.

Agni came near the Yaksha and introduced himself as the powerful god capable of burning off anything that touches him.

The Yaksha said with false surprise, 'Is that right?' Then he picked up a small dry grass and said, 'Can you burn this?'

Agni, drowned in his ego, laughed, 'Ha! Ha! Ha! You must be kidding!'

Yaksha calmly replied, 'Why don't you try it?'

Agni took the grass in his hand and tried to burn it. But strangely enough, he could do nothing. He soon returned to the party without telling anyone what happened. He couldn't help but wonder, 'Who is he?'

After a while, Indra asked the wind god Pavan to go to the Yaksha and find out the reason of his visit.

When Pavan approached the Yaksha, the Yaksha asked him, 'Who are you?'

'I am Pavan, the wind god,' he said. 'I can blow everything away when I want to.'

'Really!' said the Yaksha and gave him the small blade of grass to blow away. 'Could you blow away this blade of grass?'

Pavan could not even believe that anyone would challenge his power with a blade of dry grass. He callously put the grass on his palm and blew on it. To his utter shock, it stayed exactly as he had placed it on his palm and had not moved. He tried repeatedly to blow it away and finally gave up. Ashamed of his inability to stir a small blade of grass, he sneaked away.

Then Indra came himself. As he approached the Yaksha, it disappeared and there stood a woman. She was none else than Indra's conscience (self-acquired knowledge), who was called Uma.

'Did you see the Yaksha standing here?' asked Indra.

Uma said, 'Indra, being the king of the gods you could not recognise the messenger of Brahma, the Yaksha? The Yaksha carried the message that Brahma is the one and only source of power and none else. He taught you to be humble and to stay away from the ego that destroys you. You have had enough celebration for your victory over the Ashuras, and now return to the duties entrusted upon you by Brahma.'

The gods were ashamed of their foolish behaviour. They returned to their senses and peace once again was restored on earth.